VIA FOLIOS 89

Schistsong

Annie Rachele Lanzillotto

BORDIGHERA PRESS

Library of Congress Control Number: 2013940585

Printed in the United States.

Published by
Bordighera, Inc.
John D. Calandra Italian American Institute
25 West 43rd Street, 17th Floor
New York, NY 10036

VIA Folios 89
ISBN 1-59954-052-4
ISBN 978-1-59954-052-8

Forse sogniamo quasi abbastanza

Perhaps we dream nearly enough

for
Audrey Lauren Kindred

Contents

PART II

Your Eye You Keep on the Ball

PART III

**All Will Be Forgotten
'Cept This Gold Light We Made Together**

Acknowledgments

Poetry in this book has been published in the following:

"Ballad for Joe Zito," in *Philadelphia Poets*, Volume 19, edited by Rosemary Petracca Cappello, Philadelphia, Pennsylvania. 2013

"My Heart is Crushed Tomatoes," in *Philadelphia Poets*, Volume 19, edited by Rosemary Petracca Cappello, Philadelphia, Pennsylvania. 2013

"Spirit Track," in *2 Bridges Review*, edited by George Guida, Brooklyn, New York. 2012

"The Smiling Iceman," in *Philadelphia Poets*, Volume 18, edited by Rosemary Petracca Cappello, Philadelphia, Pennsylvania. 2012

"Mangiamange," in *Philadelphia Poets*, Volume 18, edited by Rosemary Petracca Cappello, Philadelphia, Pennsylvania. 2012

"To Be Or Not To Be ItalianaMerican," in *Women and Performance: A Journal of Feminist Theory*, guest edited by Yael Raviv, Routledge, Taylor, and Francis, UK. 2012

"Jumpin With Joy," in *Occupy Poetry*, edited by Stephen J. Boyer, Zuccotti Park, Occupy Wall Street Library, New York City. 2011

"Ballad For Joe Zito," in *Remember The Triangle Fire Coalition Online Commemorative Centennial Archive*, www.rememberthetrianglefire.org. 2011

"My Grandmother's Hands," in *Philadelphia Poets*, Volume 17, edited by Rosemary Petracca Cappello, Philadelphia, Pennsylvania. 2011. Awarded 2nd Place for the John and Rose Petracca and Family Award, judged by Nathalie Anderson.

"Manhattan Schist," in *Philadelphia Poets*, Volume 15, edited by Rosemary Petracca Cappello, Philadelphia, Pennsylvania. 2009 Awarded 2nd Place for the John and Rose Petracca and Family Award, judged by Eileen Spinelli.

"How To Cook a Heart," in *Invisible Culture: An Electronic Journal for Visual Culture*, Issue 14, Aesthetes and Eaters–Food and the Arts, guest edited by Paula Pinto, Rochester, New York. 2009

"The Fishman/ Il Pescivendolo" in *Philadelphia Poets*, Volume 15, edited by Rosemary Petracca Cappello, Philadelphia, Pennsylvania. 2009

"My Heart is Crushed Tomatoes," in *Alimentum Menu Poems*, edited by Esther Cohen, Nashville, Tennessee. 2009

"How to Catch a Flyball in Oncoming Traffic" and "How to Cook a Heart," in *Hidden New York: A Guide to Places That Matter*, edited by Marci Reaven and Steve Zeitlin, Rivergate Books, Rutgers University Press, New Jersey and London. 2006

"Strike One," in *Italian American Writers on New Jersey*, edited by Jennifer Gillan, Maria Mazziotti Gillan, and Edvige Giunta, Rutgers University Press, New Jersey and London. 2003

"The Doctor's Touch," in *Women, Health, and Medicine: Transforming Perspectives and Practice*, *Women's Studies Quarterly*, Volume XXXI, Numbers 1 & 2, Spring/Summer. Guest Editors: Alice J. Dan, Sue V. Rosser, Edvige Giunta. 2003

"Breathing in Brooklyn," in *Rising*, Volume 30, edited by Tim Wells, London. 2002

"Triple Bypass," in *The Milk of Almonds*, edited by Edvige Giunta and Louise DeSalvo, Feminist Press, New York City. 2000

"Triple Bypass," Awarded 1st Place in Poetry, in the 1st annual Anne and Henry Paolucci Prize, by the Italian American Writers Association. Judge: Maria Mazziotti Gillan. 1998

Graziemille

James W. Head III, Suzy Wahmann, Alina Lundry, Jude Rubin, Ellyne Skove, Ron Raider, Joanna Clapps Herman, Lucia Mudd, Edvige Giunta, Anthony Tamburri, Fred Gardaphè, Lisa Cicchetti, Valerie Reyes Jiminez-Roche, Rosemary Cappello, Adeel Salman, Rose Imperato, Full House Printing www.fullhouseprinting.com

Introduction

Schistsong, Annie Lanzillotto's astounding collection of poems is big and dense and speaks in a New York accent forged in the bedrock that predates the history of this great City, the metamorphic rock that is older than New York, older than Italy, many millions of years old. "Find your inner schist," your bedrock, this poet urges. Sprinkled with liberal handfuls of shiny mica, these poems are meant to kick and stomp and make sure you know they're here. They come direct from the "heel of the boot" as it was planted in the Bronx, New York.

Like Lanzillotto I grew up in the Bronx "playing in traffic." Somehow we were always aware that below the traffic was the rock, the firmament which contains the geography, geology, topography of New York. This was encoded in our bodies like DNA. "I am an American," Lanzillotto proclaims, "born on the mainland. The Bronx." The only such borough yet we have to remind ourselves that the Bronx is in America "if you call the Bronx America." Perhaps this is due to the fact that the Bronx is built not on schist but on gneiss estimated to be even older than schist, one billion years old and responsible for creating the continent. Playing in traffic "with a car coming at you" implies danger, the assumed risk in everyday living. Life is a dare. "Nobody ever expected us to walk away," Lanzi says. Survival is never certain, "because of reasons," but is a gift that must be wrested from impossible circumstances time and again. Add in Italianness, Italian-American, Bronx-Italian, *Barese*-Bronx-Italian and so forth. "Keep ya mout' shut," Lanzillotto tells us in her first book, *L is for Lion: an italian bronx butch freedom memoir* (SUNY Press 2013). An early lesson in *omertà*. Keep the silence. Do not speak. Do not tell. In our culture those who break this code of silence are shunned. Or worse. Writing, therefore, is an act of courage, bravery, strength. To become the tale-teller, the-one-with-the-mouth, to break silence is a right one can only confer upon oneself. The writer must be "made of stone" not given to cracks and fissures, strong enough not to fracture under the pressure to remain silent. The writer/witness is the antidote to the not-witness—the person who sees but doesn't say anything. We remain rooted to our ancestors, our voice, our accent, our living and our dead. "I make deals with god/all my saints pull strings for me."

As Joseph Campbell famously said, "the psychotic drowns in the same waters in which the mystic/poet swims with delight." *Schistsong* provides a great poetry festival—a Port Authority sized hangout with a cast of characters that includes: the Queens Giant, Mr. Cinquand, Rosalie whose "good eye sees rainbows," Joe Zito Triangle Fire Hero, Mother Cabrini, Rhoda Shapiro, Ulek Tosher. Emma Lazarus makes an appearance as does "little Rosie Grasso," who died at age sixteen in the Triangle Fire. Annie's Grandma, who like mine, lived in the "dark with beings." Aunt Apollonia and Uncle Gus speak from these poems and Lorenza sits, strong as stone, glass balls at her feet. Icons walk these pages like tragic saints: The Smiling Iceman, The Fishman/*Il Pescivendolo*, the Butcher, Lanzi the Soldier/Marine. These poems will teach you survival skills such as: how to cook a heart, how to approach a basketball court, how to catch a fly ball in oncoming traffic, how to wake a Marine, how to dig a foxhole, how to test batteries, and when to call on the Queer Kiss. Among her louds, Lanzillotto is out and proud, a long-time activist and early member of ACT-UP. She reveres the "hands of the field"; her grandmother's hands which held such secrets and mourns "the disappearing hands," the loss of ancient skills in our modern life. Of course we are sick: weak in body and mind, even how to eat we have forgotten. We need garlic and greens plucked from fields. And in her father's hands, "in black and white," was "the history of New York, etched in forever." There is history in this poetry; the history of rock, the history of migration, oral history, New York City history, Italian American history as in *One Hundred and Eighteen Dagoes* and music history, all filtered and recorded in this strong Bronx *Nooyawk* voice, this pre-hip hop, pre J-Lo, sparkling plain Bronx IA speech which sounds as clear as *l'acqua minerale* to my New York ear. "My accent is a relic," Lanzillotto declares; the very reason it is so important to record.

Lanzillotto has described *Schistsong* as an answer to Walt Whitman's *Leaves of Grass*. There are many overlapping elements and plenty will be written about this, and there is one striking difference. Whitman's "Mannahatta" was a welcoming place, a place to come to for freedom and democracy, a place of arrival. While that shiny promise still glitters/beckons, Lanzillotto's New York has become a "merciless" city who scorns her own. The poet vows, "I take you New York City to be my lawfully wedded," but the City answers, "I do evict you from this day forward." New Yorkers are banished from their own city for much the same reasons our ancestors were banished from Italy: for not having. "Broadway beneath Broadway," like a childhood monster come to life, can get you at any time. The American dream is not a *fait accompli* but must be earned, passed on, made brick by difficult brick. "*Barese* bones are in these bricks/*Barese* names are every building."

Audre Lorde could have been thinking of Lanzillotto when she wrote, "Poetry is not a luxury." The outer boroughs remain outer; "success" measured in comfort and glitter can be elusive. This poetry, with rhythm song and dance, as glorious as a Spaldeen flying over a brick building, is that kind of necessary. "Core to crust," Lanzillotto hands us this urban songline of our City of Glitter. This modern-day bard, risen from the Bronx, storyteller, gatherer, singer, composer, orator, drummer, flower-maker, this *cantastoria extraordinaire* records and shares her story, no holds barred, in this collection of "gorgeous drama."

ROSETTE CAPOTORTO
New York City, 2013

PART I

The Buried Sun Inside Me

Manhattan Schist

New York has a destiny of glitter.
We're built on it. Born of it. Born of glitter.
This is Manhattan schist.
This is why we can build high into the sky.
This is why cranes thread the sky,
hoist steel up into clouds.
It's cool. I press my forehead down to it.
It's alive. I breathe it in.

Four hundred and fifty million years ago,
the east coast slammed into the Atlantic sea floor,
the sand and clay dove nine miles down
into the very alive bone marrow
of this earth, hot marrow
where sand and clay
mixed with quartz and feldspar and mica and hornblende,
quartz and feldspar and mica and hornblende.
Mica, from the Latin *micare* to glitter,
Mica is atomically flat and alive,
So flat you can make a mirror out of it.
Mica loves water. Mica seeks the sea.
Mica fostered life forms before cell walls existed.
Before cell walls existed!
Thousands of degrees of heat,
megatons of pressure
Voila! Out of this glittering womb
is born the metamorphic rock: the glittering Manhattan schist!
Rock that's black and sparkles,
rock that Nooyawkahs emulate
in our slick dress and shine.

Metamorphosis is change in form.
Change by pressure, change by heat, change by friction
change by distortion, change by pressure.
The pressure we know as Nooyawkahs.
Nooyawk for Nooyawkahs.

Change is the bedrock on which we stand.
Metamorphosis is the bedrock of the walk of our life.

Our beloved Manhattan schist is a glittering skyline beneath us.
At Ground Zero it's eighteen feet below the surface.
That's why we build there high into the sky.
Schist dives deep,
two hundred and sixty feet below Village sidewalks,
comes up at midtown,
that's why we build there high into the sky.
Dives down again and surfaces uptown.
At 120th and Madison, schist is three stories high
like a whale breaking the flat-as-earth sea.
In Inwood there are glittering caves.
Skyscraper beneath skyscraper
Skyline beneath skyline
Broadway beneath Broadway
Light beneath lights
Strongest rock in the world.

You gotta find your inner schist
like the buried sun inside you.
When your crust goes to your core
and your core to your crust.
When you lose all surface accoutrements.
When you got nothin' left.
You find your inner glitter
And you know you're home.

It's great to go to Sloan-Kettering all the time.
Over the past twenty-nine years, I average sixty visits a year.
The great thing is they turn me inside out.
Blood and bile, vomit and bone marrow,
Chemo is a jute rope pulled through me.
Radiation I swallow then spit at the scum in the crosswalk,
superhero radioactive venom spit.
"Get back Asshole. You don't want me spitting on you!
I ain't kidding. Stay away from me. Toxic Lesbians Unite!"

Yellow and black radioactive trefoil symbol
I wear as an armband. The pregnant
stay outside my eight foot radius.
I can't hug my own dog.
No one can sit on my lap without reprisal.
Hell, if anyone holds me at night,
they'd absorb more radiation than one should in a lifetime.
Back off. Radiation is planted
in seeds under my skin. Radiation I take in
through every pore of skin across my whole body surface.
I turn inside out.
My crust goes to my core.
My core to my crust.
Crust to core. Core to crust.
Inner schist glitters.
The buried sun inside me.
I know I'm home
in the sidewalk's spark at night, curbs jumpin'
glittery sparks of internal light
like the buried sun in the earth we mistake for gold.

New York City glitters wherever I step
The Sun's hands sit as if some Goddess spits on each stone.
Sparks fly into the night, silver fish
awaken, sidewalks pulse and buckle.
I run over coursing waters hot molten belly. Jump
I follow the glittery spark internal light. Jump
Glittering womb that is home. Jump
My home glitters.
Glitter is my home.

I New York City, Vows

I wanna be an old lady, black cane stuck in a sidewalk groove
like a needle on an LP as I circle my block,
listening to the same nine stories kick
bellies of blue corner mailboxes
revelations from recent demolitions,
palimpsest ghost words on brick walls,
love stories on old corners,
street directions set by the course of two rivers.

I wanna be an old lady in New York City,
take a night class in Religious Studies at NYU,
watch a Magnani film at MOMA and
tell the young people "Shuush,"
when she's about to give birth on the hill.
I wanna whisper, "there's a red lighthouse
tucked atop blessed schist under the GW Bridge,"
as I stir it all away in the oldest coffee house on MacDougal,
fire in the base of the wall, with one spoon
silver around every knuckle,
Isis wings from the jeweler stabbed to
death, was it just a decade ago?

I wanna peek at the unchanged rock in caisson sinkings.
I wanna get married to New York City.
I want New York City to take me for life.
I take you, New York City
to be my lawfully wedded
to have and hold from this day forward
for better or worse for richer or poorer
in sickness and in health in good times and in bad
'til death do us—
I vow to stay passionate
to walk filled with courageous breast
to fight the wholesale erasure of culture
to not watch idly as Coney Island gets washed to sea

to write, to speak, to make performance
to give a ffffhuck.

I New York City do evict you from this day forward.
Take your queer butch ass back to Yonkers,
and call it YoHo if it makes you feel better.
Sleep on your mother's floor, outside my city limits
Go! North of the rivers! Across the rivers!
To the north! To the west!
Go to the mainland! Go south if you want to!
Go east! Pass the oceans.
I release you and your lovers.
Go find a lover with a lease, a lover with a deed,
A lover who built a straw bale house on a mountain or in the desert
A sea level lover on a houseboat,
in a shelter, cellblock. Hell.
Go back to whatever cave you crawled out of—

I New York City do seek
the rich, the healthy, the lucky, the three-generation white,
the white polite who want to come pursue a dream up my asshole
who will give me all
her energy, her money, all I want.
And who will love to be devoured
in the fire of my breathing eyes.

I New York City give you
seduction beyond your wildest dreams.
the highest highs, the lowest lows,
I New York City do take
your fertile years do take
your energy do leave you penniless.
I New York City do give you,
New York born, and born elsewhere alike,
enough food stamps. I New York City will not be said to starve.
I New York City do give indifference

enough to provide you your freedom to walk unnoticed.
I New York City do not judge you, do not I house you?

I New York City will provide you
with incessant fresh blood,
fresh food enough strips of sunlight
to see night born of day, sunsets at the waters' edge
cultural freedom, a parade once a year
Laws! So you can sleep with your window unlocked ajar
and seek retribution in the morning.

I give you people with a peopled past,
ghosts from days gone by:
Lady Mephistopheles in a red gown in The Palace of Illusions,
as handcuffs come toward her,
a man called The,
Emma Lazarus, Antonietta Pasqualicchio, little Rosie Grasso,
Jack McGurk adventure, mischief, carbolic acid
apéritifs all you like,
The Bouwerie of then, The Bowery of now,
The Bowery of tomorrow.

I New York City give you night,
when I dress in my finest shine,
I stand behind you for your photos,
I give you oxygen enough to keep you panting,
Heat through my sewer caps and grates,
You can open your *cannellini* and heat it right up on my slick skin.
Sweet tobacco air, I give you
ways and means to cure yourself. Hospitals abound.
But it will not be easy.
You must strive. You must find your inner Trump,
You must beat out the rest, in traffic, you must cut others off,
For subway seats, glaze your glance
You must pay for metered time.
Time is metered. Twenty-five cents for ten minutes
Time is unforgiving.

The clock smells your waste.
To keep your heart beating you must pay

I the city have all you need
I the city vow to push
you to not let you rest
My surface curves so not even your coffee cup can settle
on my grid. Spikes adorn my ledges
so you stay standing into the night
or fall impaled.

I New York City vow to leave you behind.
Not even on my Bowery can you lay down stretched out
horizontal.
I relegate youse back to the mainland.
C'mon! We gotta balance the equation.
Send some lunatics back to the continental United States.
I New York City can't hold all the degenerate
artists homosexuals crooked teeth painters gifted fags
and all their ancestors in my wind.
What do you want from me, housing all your life?
If I give you five years you'll want ten.
You must pay with your life.
You must pay with your blood spill on sidewalk,
Give me your unborn.

I New York City do banish you, New Yorker.
Go! Take your accent and flee.
Not even your corpse has a place within
the walls of this city.

The Absence of Red

I am lifting the city above the streetlights
where I can't hear the din of the traffic or church bells,
just the lullaby of the stream of lights alongside the East River.
I want to go to my mother's and rest.
My mother's still alive. And she'll still hand wash my underwear
and dry them in the oven.
We got a word for that,
if in your forties and you go back to living with ya mother,
i Bombocioni.
I know, I know, everything sounds better than what it is,
in Italian.
Even heart attack. *Attaco di cuore.*
Even heart attack sounds romantic.

I grew up in the Bronx, playing in traffic
on a one-way street named after a Saint.
I never knew what three miracles were attributed to him
or what favors he leaned on granting.
Stoop. Sidewalk. Street.
That was the progression of my entrance into the world.
You learn your lessons early.
When I was three, I sat on the stoop
and watched the boys in all their freedom,
zooming up and down the block,
peeling their t-shirts up over their heads
and tucking them in the backs of their dungarees,
whacking Spaldeens with their stickball bats,
sending Spaldeens far into the sun.

At five I got to play on the sidewalk.
I'd go to the corner to climb the mailbox on Zerega
where this junkie sat under a black hat
melting in a puddle of sunlight, "I'm Jesse James."

At seven my mother allowed me to cross the street on my own,
and to play in the street. That's where the stickball game happened.

In the middle of the street the lane of sky was so big.
I knew I'd never see a sky any bigger than that.
I remember the traffic light green
was busted, so, I crossed in the absence of red
and hoped I didn't get killed. I ran across.
Life felt like being in the middle of the street ever since.
Crossing in the absence of red.

This is the Bronx

Worked all my life.
Haven't taken a vacation since I was twelve.
Learned to drive at eight years old.
You know how I learned to drive?
You know how I learned to drive?
My father puts me on the truck.
He says Drive
I say Pop I can't drive.
So he socks me.
He says Drive.
And I drove.
Not only that, I backed out the driveway.
Learned how to drive in reverse.
That's my life in a nutshell.
Driving in reverse.

The Queens Giant

Colonialization? Eh, that was a cure for Continental Drift.
White men reunited the land masses,
Went everywhere they could figure out how to get to,
Every nook and cranny in the universe,
Where there was a wind they lifted a sail
Yeah, they get lost, that's how they get where they were going,
Named whole continents after themselves,
Rivers and islands, after their shipmates.

On the corner over there used to be a butcher.
There were five butchers from Prince to Houston.
Now there's only one. Old Moe.
He never got air conditioning.
You go in there it smells like a butcher shop is supposed to smell.
Attract flies smell.
The whole street used to smell like that.
Every one of us is just a fly to meat.

On that corner was Bella's Cafe.
Before that, the live chicken market.
This corner had horses just up from the firehouse.
We all have the same story, since Continental Drift,
Since Mohawk and Lenape and Wickquasgeck walked
Down from ice shelf Siberia.
Since Continental Pangea when you could walk
Europe to Africa to America cause that was just here to there.
Flowers walked,
Animals walked, rocks,
Everything that sang walked.
Take away the water, you still could walk.
Continents pull apart, push, mash up into mountains and coves.
Tectonic plates shift, crash, dive.
Manna Hatta.
Island of hills. The place where the sun was born.
Why does anyone leave New York?
See that tulip tree?

They call her "The Queens Giant."
The oldest living tree. She's the one survivor
To witness all New York City,
To breathe in all the stories from the Matinecock
to the Dutch to the L.I.E..
Here she stands, where she exhaled colonists,
Cars, First Peoples, forests.
How sweet
the air.

The Fishman / *Il Pescivendolo*
Hughes Avenue & 187th Street, Bronx

Mr. Cinquand hasn't spoken for three months.
Puppetta feeds hard candy to her dogs.
Rosalie's one eye is all closed and the good eye sees rainbows.
Amelia is a shut in.
Beppe calls his girls by his sons' names.
Still we go on.
There's a thousand years here if you count us all up.
People are living too long these days.
It's not modern medicine keeping us alive it's spite
we stay alive on spite.
I wonder if it's because of that fish man.
    "U pesce! U pesce!"   Fish! Fish!
He knew how to sell. He cried an incantation over the whole block.
At the sound of his call shutters opened,
    "Sto qua signorr!   I am here, Madam!
    Cosa vuoi 'sta mattin!?   What would you like this morning?
    Signora! Va scendere!"   Madam, come down!
He asked you what it is you wanted.
He'd make you promises.
He'd tell you who eats fish never dies.
    "Chi mangi pesce mai morite!"
He had a fish just for you, from the center of the sea,
All your relatives would be sane after eating his fish.
Your cast iron pan would age with a thousand minerals.
Aunt Zia's eyes would uncross.
You would never die you would never die.
    "Bella mi! U pesce U pesce freschc'. Ven aca!
    Chi mangi pesce muore mai. Chi mangi pesce muore mai."
Cutting fish, reciting prayers, a sandwich of money in his pocket,
What he didn't sell, he cooked, he
canned, who knows what he did with all that fish.
I wonder if that's why we're all living so long in this neighborhood.
Puppetta. Amelia. Rosalie. Mr. Cinquand. Beppe.
Still we go on.

The Smiling Iceman
166th Street and Melrose Avenue, Bronx

All of a sudden nobody needs ice
and they forget your father's name.
Ice was twenty-five cents a cake.
The people needed three, four cakes.
Back then it was a chunk of the Hudson.
A ways up, the Hudson turns fresh.
That's where the ice harvest used to happen.
They'd cut the river up with a handsaw
and bring all the ice up and down all the stairs.

Ice! Ice! Ice! Ice!
Up and down all the dumbwaiters.
It was his hands had the rope burns.
He was up at four and never down,
because the work was never done.
Now you don't remember his name?
Every cake, each ice!
Every frame of sidewalk!
Barese bones are in these bricks,
Barese names are every building.
Fish born into an ocean end up in a bucket,
Rivers end up cross-cut to fit some old lady's icebox.

Never made a soap that could take the grease off my father's hands.
It was all there in black and white, the history of New York
etched in forever; palms, knuckle-skin and beneath his finger nails.
By the time he was twelve he earned
the nickname the Smiling Iceman.
A three hundred pound block of ice altar
skidded down a wooden chute
into the pointed tongs like fangs of a soldier half that weight
cracked teeth, battle sores on his feet and dreams
His nights shook
The enemy hid in his grey matter,
At four a.m. he shouldered ice

As if the crystal frozen weight could heal all his wounds eternal
He stared into the spinning cold sun
A prism of block ice on his Bronx shoulder, strong as hell,
Visions melt,
Those that don't freeze up inside.

Ice heals wounds.
Mark it on the ice, Joey, mark it
on the ice
and smile.

Triple Bypass

Non è posso che mai più ci vedremo faccia a faccia.
It's not possible that we will never see each other again, face to face.

You have to understand the basics to survive a whole life.
"L'arancia di mattina—oro puro; nel pomeriggio—argento;
di sera—piombo."
Mamma never had an ice cold drink 'til she was nineteen
and in America.
Water, wine and a squeeze of the goat whenever she had a cold.
Hank didn't listen.
"If you call the Bronx America," was all he said to me,
Licking the last malt off his lip.

If she sang to herself while her fingers pulled my shoelaces tight
I knew I had a good chance of getting an ice-cream cone
outside the slaughterhouse.
I held my mouth full of cream
'til it dissolved as her arm dove into cages
where feathers became her hand.
Her face reddened and her mouth gathered spit to knock
the price down. Feathers everywhere
as she pointed at the chicken whose breast
passed her inspection. Feathers in my mouth as its blood fell
into a pail. *"A spezzia!"* she sang triumphantly.
Onward we marched up and down the market aisles,
hunting and gathering, feeling the heads of lettuces
like the skulls of babies, feeling
for the soft spot, smelling each peach at a microphone's distance,
remembering something there, then moving on,
pocketing garlic, pocketing parsley.
Some things in life you shouldn't pay for.
"L'aglio è essenziale. L'aglio è l'essenza della vita."
I tried to tell Hank.
Garlic will straighten you out, if you know how to eat it.
Garlic will push an ocean through your aorta.
Sammy he ate fried foods.
Vinny was a *sopressata* man.

And Hank loved milkshakes.
We all had the same operation, the American
senior citizen bar mitzvah.
They were all dead in six months.
Me?
I'm not really here.
I'm on borrowed time.
I boil everything.

Mangiamange

Throgs Neck, Bronx

In memory of Lorenza on the loss of her sons:
Nicola, Giuseppe, Luigi, Lorenzo, RIP August 5th, 1939

Get on line to kiss her hello.
Once one each cheek.
The second kiss in deference to where we come from.
She crossed an ocean,
Made the scorched earth give birth,
Married a man and learned to love him.
Buried four sons after the garage exploded,
Insisted the women believe the explosion was an accident.
But men, men get their messages elsewhere.

She sits in a chair.
Every time you see her she is in this chair.
Her chair is in line with a runway at La Guardia.
The planes still pass overhead.
The chair is all crushed blood velvet and deep mahogany
Tall, straight back and stiff arms with glass balls.
She holds onto these balls.
She says very little
but what she does say comes straight from her heart,
forget vocal chords, just heart riding on air,
"*Mangiamange. Mangiamange.*"
She points a butterscotch ball up at you from across the room.
The silver candy dish, at attention by her side,
filled with butterscotch balls.
In her lap, butterscotch colored cellophanes
like shiny fallen leaves twisted tightly.

The whole kitchen turns upside down
as you stare under her chair
into the crystal ball glass feet clasped by mahogany claws.
Women cook and men look
into green screens and teletype machines
decoding messages from overseas.

Words hammering on paper rolling up into men's hands words
span the pages and steam
streams down from the white tin ceiling into the hand
the wooden spoon circles the great aluminum pot.
Women circle new knives and forks about the table.
Sliced peaches like goldfish in wine.
Blood levels meniscus tilt in clear glasses.
A white bedspread shakes the wind out back
by the pigeon coop. Pigeons find the shortest routes home,
Their racing times punch-coded into a secret brass clock.
Across the street, Saint Raymond's Cemetery,
where all of us this side of the Atlantic return
to Bronx earth
cold solemn marble slab facts,
the longest spellings of our names,
and above the house,
a plane already with its wheels down.

Open your eyes.
She's the most beautiful corpse you've ever seen.
Silver shoes, hair spun white, fingernails gold
and on her lace chest a diamond crucifix
between breasts more pert than ten decades allow.
Rings of red roses in tight explosions surround her.

Unlike the Rose

Unlike the rose
the heart is woven
Unlike the sun
the heart has walls
The sun you can fall into
the sun without a skin
Unlike the heart
Unlike the rose

Non Come la Rosa

Non come la rosa
il cuore è intrecciato
Non come il sole
il cuore ha le muri
Il sole è posso caduto dentro
Il sole senza la pelle
Non come il cuore
Non come la rosa

Mom on Lorenza: Verbatim

These women were made of stone.
When I say stone, I mean strong.
Not cement.
Cement cracks.
Stone doesn't crack.
When I say stone,
I don't mean they were cold unfeeling people.
I'm simply referring to strength.
Cement is manmade.
Stone wears down around the edges.
On the outside.
It becomes weather-beaten.
Stone doesn't crack.
You have to explode it.
Cement will crack from wear.
It's a mixture of different things.
Stone will last, you know,
almost forever.
You actually have to dynamite it.

Asthma and the Feast
Little Italy, New York City

I had an asthma attack at the Feast of San Gennaro,
Uncle Gus yanked me through the crowd,
tucked a ten dollar bill inside the Blessed Mary's dress
as if she were a common whore floating up Mulberry Street.
He didn't notice I wasn't breathing.
"You havin fun You havin fun You havin fun!"
"Whaddyawant whaddyawant whaddyawant!"
I inhaled powdered sugar off the *zeppoli*
and looked for something to want.
"I like the white cowboy hat."
"The one on the guy's head?"
"Yea, the one on the guy's head."
"Mista, how much for ya hat!"
Uncle Gus loved this Street.
He could make anything happen
with a magic word and hand motion.
"Mista, how much for ya hat!"
"It ain't for sale."
I stepped away. Uncle Gus tugged me back.
He had something to teach me.
He gave the guy in the hat a slow handshake
A smiling word in the guy's ear.
The man promptly took the hat off his head and handed it over.
Uncle Gus put it on my head.
"Remember," he said to me, "every thing has a price tag."

O! to handshakes IN GOD WE the eye over the pyramid TRUST
and one God's name folded tight
like a prayer in the palm of Uncle Gus's hand,
A prayer pushed in a crack in the wall.
Up the dress of *la Madonna* with a ten dollar bill.
No disrespect.

Italian Italians

This is the house Marconi
sent the first U.S. ship to shore messages.
This is the house where sixty residents live
in various stages of brain trauma.
For a few hours I take my father out,
and we go for a walk by the water.
Out the red basement door of the mental home,
up three cement steps.
Two coffees black to go.
We stare into the rocking silence of the Atlantic
where the fishermen come into Babylon.
There's a hook on the pier set up like a hangman's launch,
for catch bigger than humans.

Looking east past the grey bridge ethereal skeleton to Fire Island,
I think of my cousins in Italy
and how our destinies would have been reversed
had the ocean swung on its brass hinge in the opposite direction.
We are Italian. We think of our cousins in Italy as Italian Italians.
The ocean is a beveled mirror
in which we imagine each other's lives
and have distorted visions of our own.

When I first met my cousins, our eyes locked,
bodies hugged and we cried,
unable to translate to each other any truth about our lives but this:
You are my cousin. I've dreamed of you all my life knowing
our lives could have been reversed.
I could have grown up a *Contadina*,
and you coulda ran the Bronx streets
had our fates not been reversed in 1919,
when Great Grandmother Rachele's finger wavered
like the needle of a compass, settling all of our destinies
as it passed over the head of the *vent'uno* old Maria
and settled on *dici'nove* young Rosina.
Thus plotting the charts for their courses and all of ours.

You go. You go instead my child. *Figghe migghe, si va invece.*
The Great War interrupted the plan.
Maria was was deemed too old post-war to make a new go of life.

The Atlantic taps and waves
but the concrete pier stays seemingly immovable.
My father pulls out a Lucky Strike with his teeth
and lights it in the cup of his hands.
The red band floats out to sea.
He's softer now that he's half of what he once was.
And me, I am thirty and strong enough finally
to kill him.

To Be or Not To Be ItalianaMerican
1ˢᵗ Avenue and St. Marks Place, New York City

'Scarole and spiNACH were two dollars cheaper than broccoli rabe
stating a hierarchy of greens I didn't understand.
Vesteddi sandwiches were the cheapest at a buck ninety-five
which suited my pocket but I didn't know what it was
so I asked and thought, Hell, I didn't grow up eating spleen,
I don't even have a spleen.
I never saw eels in my bathtub,
never spread bone marrow on toast
nor marinated a head of any kind.
Never saw the goat's eyes cry,
never saw goats' eyes
never saw goats.
Never saw boiling eyes cry.
I fell
off the flat earth.
My Bronx was the flat earth
paved by my concrete thoughts.
I pirate myself.
I play myself.
I buy fat speckled ham.
I chop the ends offa words.
My hands filled with blood do all the talking.
I am hungrier than you can ever imagine.
Famished.
You I curse.
I make deals with God.
All my saints pull strings for me.
If you come too close,
I'll put a scapular around your neck.
I am ItalianaMerican.
I shop in the morning and I cook all day.
I look you in the eye. Pour concrete.
Frittatas fill my pocketbooks.
I wipe surfaces for germs that live to attack me.
Money I hide rolled in a pipe in the basement.

Don't cook for me.
Don't mispronounce my *formaggio* or DiMaggio.
Don't expand my world
so my ancient greatness loses focus in mine eye.
I fell
off the flat earth.
I flatten the earth everyday with my paved thoughts.
I get colonoscopies on Columbus Days,
back to back with my mother.
I open my anus up for the camera.
My mother tells the handsome doctor,
"Don't discover nothing new.
Columbus discovered enough."
The anesthetist is a cutie. She says, "Here's your Piña Colada,"
as she pushes milky white Propafol into my one good vein.
I pull my head up for ten seconds of bliss
before I black out and shout,
"You all should do a reality show. New York Ass
hoooooooooles."

Eels swarm in my bathtub.
Marrow saturates my toast.
A head marinates for me
as we speak
goat's eyes cry
as I fall
off
the flat
flat
earth.

My Grandmother's Hands

This is my hand.
This is my grandmother's hand.
My grandmother grew up holding crops.
I grew up holding crap, things that never lasted.
This is the difference between us.
Sneakers I flung up to telephone wires
while figs came into her hands.
My grandmother handles every thing like there's a life inside it.
Even plastic! Plastic, she holds like an egg!
There is life inside it.
Plastic, she holds like it grew right out of the ground
I'm standing on!

Watch the disappearing hands.
Guarda le mani che scompaiono.
These hands you never see in America.
Queste mani mai visto in L'America.
Hands of the fields, are hands!
Le mani delle campagna, è la mano!
Hands of the fresh air, are hands!
Le mani dell'aria fresca, è la mano!
Hands of the horse, are hands!
Le mani dello cavallo, è la mano!
Today everything is made by machine. Nothing is made by hand.
Oggi tutto fanno per la industria. Niente ha fatto di mano.

This is my hand.
This is my grandmother's hand.
You know how her hands were made?
From the kitchen to the fields, from the kitchen to the fields,
from the kitchen to the fields to the kitchen.
To the kitchen she carried,
she carried water dead chickens and eggs.
Water dead chickens and eggs and this
is my grandmother's hand.
This is my hand.

It's the life that makes the hand.
Her hands have eggs inside them.
My hands cannot make what her hands make.
My hands open books.

Nonna! Show my hands to make the little circles!
Show my hands to flick *cavateel* so they jump
like grasshoppers off fingertips!
Guarda! Queste mani che scompaiono! Guarda!
Watch! The disappearing hands! Watch!

In the Dark

Grandma wasn't alone like the rest of us.
She sat in the dark.
I saw spirits around her. In the shadows
her dolls sat on the couch with their long eyelashes,
in green and yellow bustier dresses she crocheted,
her old television set, mute, tin foil wrapped antennae,
her transparent lace curtains
worn smooth and soft as veined garlic skin,
bulged with inhabitants.
Grandma lived in the dark with beings.
Curtain wind beings, fire-escape beings,
lampshade shapely beings cool as eggshells,
gas flame rings on the stove beings,
squeaky floor beings, heat knocks in the pipe beings,
beings in thick coats of paint that clogged the sockets on the walls,
and the hinges of the bathroom door
where Grandpa's leather strop still hung,
beings in the couch that exhaled when she lifted her body,
beings bubbling into the glass knob of the coffee pot.
In her apartment, I dreaded
the light of day, when ordinary objects came back into focus,
and the world turned inanimate again.
"Hey, where'd everybody go?"

My Heart is Crushed Tomatoes

I drink Chianti out of a chipped jelly jar and sit in the heat,
Stare at the peach tree branch, wide as her calves,
Grandma Rose Peach Tree.

My heart is crushed tomatoes
When my American name comes out of her mouth.
My heart is crushed tomatoes
When she tells me to be quiet.

When Grandma Rose spit in the dirt, a tree sprouted.
She spit her peach pits out my mother's living room window.
She died. *Boom!* The peach tree sprouted.
Now it's two stories tall and curved like Grandma,
Branches twisted one on top of another as her toes.

My heart is crushed tomatoes
When I prune the tree branches, snap the suckers,
saw off a branch thick as her leg.
My heart is crushed tomatoes
Squeezed through Grandma's hand,
Squeezed through the aluminum strainer.

She was ninety-nine when they wanted to cut her leg
off at the knee,
My brother said, "It's just a piece of meat."
The cardiovascular surgeon nodded his head
heavy with knowledge.
I stood up. I told them, "Give me eight days."
I lathered her leg in crushed garlic and olive oil
and sang the *Ave Maria*.
I held my hands over her blood clot and poured heat
from the palm of my hands.
I got all the women in my family to do it, some of the men too,
Sing, pray, pour heat. Eight nights in a garlic vigil,
my girlfriend Audrey and I sat there until Grandma Rose
got up and walked out of the hospital on her own two legs

the surgeon watched in silence.
A year later Grandma marched to her grave
with two legs on.
Then the peach tree sprouted.

It's another spring now
Grandma Rose is covered in pink blossoms,
the same pink as my mother's fingernail polish.
Last year she gave a thousand peaches,
Blushed gold orbs, right in through the window
into my mother's hands.

Sunsets and Supermarkets

When the sun dips so low
below the tree line
just leaving its glow

Sunsets and supermarkets make me feel sad
reminding me of things I wish I had

The song of the night
daily rhythms with Mom no more

The burning pink
is my link

to the dead
All the souls rush to my head

Sunsets and supermarkets make me feel sad
reminding me of things I wish I had

sun low
pink glow
song night
Mom no
pink link
souls so

How to Cook a Heart
Arthur Avenue and 187th Street, Bronx

Now you slice the veal heart,
A quarter of inch and you put them in the broiler.
You slice the heart this way
About a quarter of an inch,
And you put them in, like a steak.
You slice across the top
Broiled and you put some lemon on top
And you eat it like that.
You turn it a few times and you put down,
You know, brownish, and you eat it like that.
Or you chop in small pieces and you fry with lots of onions.
Put oil. Now listen.
You get a knife.
You go through the whole hearts
And you make like chunks, small chunks.
You go the other way.
Take off a little fat, and you make it in small chunks,
and you fry together, with a lot of onions.
First you put the onion, then you turn the hearts.
You put the oil, a little olive oil, a little hot pepper,
a little salt, and that's it.
And turn them. Fry 'em. Fry 'em good.
Hot pepper, olive oil, salt and onions.
Onion. A lot of onion.
White, yellow, any kind of onions.
Those the little hearts.
The veal, you fry 'em together, the lambs'
The small ones.
Then there's another way.
The two of them, you mix them together and slice them,
make them in a sauce, make a tomato sauce, like a stew.
Any kind of hearts.
Slice it, in a gravy, throw in a gravy and make 'em like a stew.
First you fry a few minutes, like five minutes.
First you brown it with garlic, olive oil, a little parsley, salt, pepper.

Fry it up.
And throw them in the gravy.
Any kind of hearts.
Those are the three ways.
Never bread a heart.
There's another way.
My mother-in-law's way.
You make a hole in the heart.
She makes it that way.
A hole in the heart.
I've had it that way.
What you do is cut the bottom of the heart.
You cut. Then you take the hole, and you chop it very small.
You cut the bottom. That's the nerves, the fat.
You throw that away.
Then you turn the heart over.
Yes, like a circle and you scoop it.
That you chop, you save.
You put it aside. Get parsley. Get Romano cheese. And garlic.
And chop it. You know, grated cheese, and you mix it
all together, cheese, garlic, parsley, and the pieces of the heart,
and you mix all together and you stuff it that way.
You put it back in the heart.
You bury it in the heart.
Put them in. Let them cook. About three fifty.
You know when it's done.
How long it takes depends on the heart.

Carry My Coffee

CHORUS
I carry my coffee baby
I carry my coffee
in the street where it's sweet
I carry my coffee
Don't go beatin my chances and grabbin my opportunities yeah
Don't go beatin my chances and grabbin my opportunities nah nah
In the street where it's sweet
I carry my coffee

VERSE I
Apollonia Lanzillotto was a donut visionary,
In the Bronx where visions necessary, to survive

After World War II, she was struck by a vision,
And like all luminaries she was met with derision.

"New Yorkers can learn to take a coffee on the go," she said, and
Everyone around her said: "No No No,
Morning coffee is drunk at home, *a casa*,
It's unheard of to take a coffee in the street and roam.
No one in their right mind drinks a coffee in the street."

And she insisted:
"New Yorkers will learn
to grab a coffee and a donut on their way to work,
In the subway, they will love, a cup of fresh perk."

CHORUS
I carry my coffee baby, I carry my coffee
In the street where it's sweet, I carry my coffee.
Don't go beatin my chances and grabbin my opportunities—yeah
Don't go beatin my chances and grabbin my opportunities—no no
In the street where it's sweet, I carry my coffee.

VERSE II
Apollonia married a tall handsome Tony.
He wore military dress for their matrimony.

Arm in arm they marched under an aisle of crossed swords,
Adopted a beautiful baby boy and thanked the lord.

Opened the donut shop in the subway in Morris Park,
Walked to work in the pre-dawn Bronx dark.

Tony had sweet eyes and a good sense of humor,
and Battle Fatigue, so goes the rumor.

World War Two was over in civilian minds.
Soldiers' sufferings, nobody recognized the signs.

Tony took a strap into the donut shop kitchen,
Hung himself on the spot, they were 'sposed to get rich in.

(beat)

Coffee and donuts—swept the nation,
Under other names profits incorporation.

It all started in the Bronx with a girl on time
The family beauty. Ooooo. What happened to her almond eyes?

CHORUS
Don't go beatin my chances and grabbin my opportunities—yeah
Don't go beatin my chances and grabbin my opportunities—no no
In the street where it's sweet, I carry my coffee
I carry my coffee baby, I carry my coffee
In the street where it's sweet. I carry my coffee

VERSE III
Apollonia broke out of Bronx State,
Jacoby and Bellevue and followed her fate.

Made a career as a Crossing Guard in the 4-3 precinct,
Saw cops in action, crooked foolish indecent.

Apollonia noticed every little thing going down,
She shot photos of cops, followed them all around town.

Gave her superiors photos of patrol cars,
Proved cops on duty, were drinking in bars.

Apollonia with her camera walked the streets of New York,
In the Bronx and Manhattan, cops started to talk.

Then one day a car came at her,
ran her down, broke both her legs.

CHORUS
Don't go beatin my chances and grabbin my opportunities—yeah
Don't go beatin my chances and grabbin my opportunities—no no
In the street where it's sweet, I carry my coffee
I carry my coffee baby, I carry my coffee
In the street where it's sweet. I carry my coffee

VERSE IV
Apollonia rose again, this time, on two crutches,
Tape wound around the handles,
she walked the streets like a homeless Duchess

I found her in Port Authority, round 1992,
she said, "I'm not myself. Life's what happens to you."

Her words rung in my ears until I stand here with you.
"I'm not myself. Life's what happens to you."
"I'm not myself. Life's what happens to you."

In her black leather cap, she still had plenty of fight,
Silver paint on her face in 8th Avenue streetlight.

Obsessed with cops, she was still on a mission,
She came a long way from that donut shoppe kitchen.

As for me, I always avoided police in the street.
But my Aunt with her camera went at them. That was her beat.

(rant)
I'm not myself I need a whole makeover.
You know 4-3 cops don't come around here no more.
I don't know why.
Look at the hole in the floor.
Look how they repaired.
I can't climb since the hit and run accident.
There's somebody in the building, controlling.
It is what it is.
Don't get funny with me.
I got the coffee maker.
Somebody was tampering.
How horrible the coffee tasted that I carry my coffee.
Would you believe it?
I carry my coffee.
You know my wristwatch is at City Hall
with two Bronx precincts inscribed on it.
I was going to the cops' reunion to see cops I worked with
in front of City Hall.
There was somebody in plain clothes who resembled a motorcycle
cop.
I'm asking him where to go for legal help.
This is before the hit and run accident.
So, then I take off my wristwatch to show him
two Bronx precincts inscribed on it.
and he's looking at it, and he's telling me where to go for legal help.
So, then I insisted I go to the cops' reunion.
There's nothing wrong with me.
I get my Pap Smear every year.
I wear wash and wear.
I always liked comforters.
They're beatin your chances and grabbin your opportunities.

Down by The Square they have someone who resembles a woman
working the bank. They remember me.
Oh, I gotta stay in this section, God, because my Boss Cop
couldn't hold off his pension with all the paperwork
about unusual current injuries.
I never resigned.
They gave me ten dollars a month food stamps.
This time a the month I'm scringing.
I need money for Secret.
The Spanish took over that house too.
She calls the I.G.
I go to Medicaid.
They give me the runaround.
I don't get reimbursed for prescriptions.
You know, it's funny.
There was a felonious assault.
Whisper! Her name is Charlotte.
I can't tolerate her.
I work at Saint Raymond's three years Castle Hill.
She's such a sneak.
That sneaky Charlotte.
All I need is a cup of ice.
I walk into the pizzeria.
I say: You know me I used to be the Crossing Guard
on the corner twenty-five years.
You see that phone booth?
You can thank me for that phone booth.
I don't think these people are still here.
I don't forget Saint Raymond's. My post.
I put a phone booth here.
I had stock. AT&T stock.
I wrote to the company that I was the only Crossing Guard
without a callbox or a phone booth.
They came down because I had stock.
That phone booth is there because a me.
That is me helping the community over here.
Because a me you have that phone booth.
Just a cup of ice, please.

CHORUS
You know 4-3 cops don't come 'round here no more.
You know 4-3 cops don't come 'round here no more.
4-3 cops don't come, 4-3 cops don't come,
4-3 cops don't come 'round here no more.

I need a whole makeover. I am not myself. (X3)

Don't get funny with me. (X8)

CHORUS
I carry my coffee baby. I carry my coffee
In the street where it's sweet. I carry my coffee
Don't go beatin my chances and grabbin my opportunities—yeah
Don't go beatin my chances and grabbin my opportunities—no no
In the street where it's sweet
I carry my coffee

Ballad for Joe Zito

Lemme tell you 'bout Joe Zito,
The kinda man you wanna know.
Selfless acts of courage were his destiny.
Elevator Man. Triangle Factory.

Born the first of September, 1883, fifteen minutes past ten.
Giuseppe Alessandro Zito, sweet green eyes,
he'd grow to be the noblest of men.
At eighteen he left Sere, *Provincia di Salerno*, Italy,
Came to *L'America*. Got a job at the Triangle Factory.
Joe ran one of two passenger elevator cars,
The other was run by a man named Gaspare Mortillaro.
But factory workers were treated as freight,
Backdoor elevators took their five hundred bodies
up to floors nine and eight.

Lemme tell you 'bout Joe Zito,
The kinda man you wanna know.
Selfless acts of courage were his destiny.
Elevator Man. Triangle Factory.

Joe and Gaspare brought to the executive floor,
bosses, foreladies, and buyers,
And in twin bowler hats, The Shirtwaist Kings:
union busters, door lockers and liars.
It was a payday in March, a Saturday night,
fifteen minutes to quittin' time,
All Hell broke loose when Joe heard "Fire!"
Glass smashing, fists bashing, way up high.
Joe glanced over at Gaspare and they locked eyes,
And without a single word, pulled their cars up to the fast fast fire
way up in the sky.
Up! Up! Up! To save lives,
all the workers were screaming, distraught.
Joe Zito never gave his own safety one single thought.

Lemme tell you 'bout Joe Zito,
The kinda man you wanna know.
Selfless acts of courage were his destiny.
Elevator Man. Triangle Factory.

Girls dove into Joe's elevator car
clutching fabric shears and scissors,
Another guy would'a minded his own biz'iness.
Italian American to the core,
Joe Zito never ran for the door.
Up! Up! Up! Joe! Joe! Joe! Into fire higher higher he climbed,
He went back up about eighteen times.
Why didn't Joe go up a nineteenth you say?
Mezzomorte at the bottom of the shaft, our noble Joe lay.
Elevator dropped, smashed at basement level.
Cables gave in to fire, an overloading hell-hole.
Jumping on Joe's car, girls after girls after girls after girls.
Caving the roof, flesh roasted, hair in ribbons and curls.
They dragged Joe out onto Washington Place half dead,
Rushed him to Saint Vincent's Hospital,
stab wounds on his arms and forehead.
What ever happened to Gaspare?
He was last seen running into the smoke filled *l'aria*.

Lemme tell you 'bout Joe Zito,
The kinda man you wanna know.
Selfless acts of courage were his destiny.
Elevator Man. Triangle Factory.

Povero Giuseppe Alessandro never recovered since he saw,
"Burning Rockets" from the eighth floor, fall.
He couldn't forget girls trapped in flames, or
Judge Crain and his gavel saying,
"Shirtwaist Kings are not to blame."
Joe left New York City in a state of deprivation,
Shell-shocked from Triangle workers' asphyxiation and
decapitations.
Scarred for life, from all he saw,

Joe headed west and seven years later, registered for the Army
during The Great War.

No rich man could buy Joe's word
His green sad eyes had saw and heard. All
the papers said he died without a penny.
No bribe could change Joe's testimony. Ah!
The Shirtwaist Kings offered thousand dollar bribes,
While the U.S. economy was taking the great dive.
Joe kept free to tell the truth.
Shirtwaist Kings got rich off insurance loot.
And like too many of our brave
Our noble Joe was buried in an unmarked grave.

Lemme tell you 'bout Joe Zito,
Italian American hero.
Selfless acts of courage were his destiny.
He saved a-hun', a-hundred fifty.
He couldn't a' dreamed *this*, when he left Italy.

Elevator Man, we sing your name.
Thanks Joe! Thanks Joe! Thanks Joe! Thanks Joe!

Girls, Girls

Girls! Girls! Teenage immigrants, tell me,
where did you work last night?
Somebody tell me. C'mon Rose, Sarah, Daisy.

Washington and Greene, in the factory, where the door
kept locked, by greed.

O Girls! Girls! Teenage immigrants, tell me,
where did you go in the fire?
Tessie, Caterina, Antonietta, somebody tell me.

I jumped to the street where my bones and concrete meet,
the sewer, my blood runs through.

Girls O Girls! Teenage immigrants, tell me,
of your New York dreams.
Rosaria, Celia, Annie, somebody tell me.

Well I ran from poverty, persecution, misery.
We were starving, needed a buck,
I got on the boat to try my luck.
Made it 'cross the sea to the wave of Liberty.
Worked the Triangle Factory, in the New York Garment Industry,
Where amber waves of flame caught me.
So I dove for the sky, broken window, promises
Spring air. I prayed, New York City, catch me!

We were body makers,
sleeve makers, sleeve setters, collar makers, cuff setters, yoke setters,
buttonhole makers, tuckers, closers, hemmers, joiners,
finishers, pressers, button sewers, lace runners,
embroidery trimmers, thread trimmers, sample makers.
Makers. Joiners. Finishers.

O Girls! Girls! Teenage immigrants, tell me,
how burning hot is greed?
C'mon tell me, Sadie, Lina, Josie, Margaret.

Well, our breath caught the fire,
hair and lace, the flames,
and cinders
became our names.

One Hundred and Eighteen Dagoes

What is it about shoe polish and cut leather that smells like home?
Or the fanning of a deck of cards between a workman's hands?
Or elbow pipe plumbing holding up a grapevine?
Or a truck tire turned inside out and cut decoratively with jagged
edges for geraniums?
Or a wall of polished brass mailboxes in a marble hallway,
each marble step worn down in the middle
where scores I will never know have tread?
Or salami sticking out of good hard bread,
and the sharp sting of provolone?
When I speak, I speak with a hundred and eighteen Dagoes
inside me.
The hundred and seventeen
I can count plus one and the legion beside them.
Eleven lynched outside the Parish House Prison
in New Orleans in 1891,
on the site of present day Congo Square:
Scaffidi, Marchesi, Monasterio, Macheca,
Polizzi, Bagnetto, Geraci, Romero,
Traina, Loretto Comitz, Caruso.
After the Police Chief was shot, his alleged dying words were,
"Dagoes did it."
Italians were rounded up *en masse*, jailed, tried.
Innocent verdicts and mistrials followed.
A mob of *prominenti*; white men, civic leaders, respected citizens,
at the Henry Clay statue on Canal Street, rallied,
took law into their own fists. Stormed the prison,
dragged Sicilians into the street, hung them from lamp posts.
Shot them down in the dirt.
A hundred years later, against Italians,
it is still murmured in the streets:
Who killa da Chief? Who killa da Chief? Who killa da Chief?
Eleven anarchists and radicals:
Nicola Sacco, Bartolomeo Vanzetti, Luigi Galliani,
Virgilia D'Andrea, Carlo Tresca, Armando Borghi,
Angela Bambace, Maria Roda, Maria Barbieri,

Ninfa Baronio, Ernestina Cravello.
One general: Giuseppe Garibaldi.
Thirteen Martyrs of Lovere: *i giustiziati*, whose death
on December 22, 1943 gave birth to Garibaldi's 53rd Brigade:
Francesco Bezzi, Vittorio Lorenzini,
Guglielmo Giacinto Macario, Giovanni Moioli,
Luca Nikitsch, Giuseppe Ravelli,
Gianni Vender, Salvatore Conti, Aleandro Locardi, Giulio Buffoli,
Ivan Piana, Mario Tognetti, Andrea Guizzetti,
One *bambina* of the massacre of Sant'Anna di Stazzema:
August 12th, 1944, Anna Pardino, twenty days old.
Sixteen nuns: the "Poor Clares," bombed
on February 10th, 1943, near Castel Gandolfo.
One Barese priest: Partigiano Don Pietro Pappagallo,
who blessed three hundred and three *partigiani*
in the caves of the Fosse Ardeatine,
before they all were executed on March 24th, 1944,
on their knees in caves,
with one Nazi bullet each
in the back of their brains. One lousy bullet each.
The least the Nazis could have done were make sure
they were all dead before the caves
were sealed with explosives.
One peacemaker lawmaker: Marcantonio,
Two hero cops: Joseph Petrosino and Michael Fischetti
of the NYPD's Italian Squad,
One hero photographer: Letizia Battaglia
who took pictures of Mafia massacres,
then years later floated the photos with *i fiori* out to sea.
Forty-three workers who jumped or choked to death
in the fire at the Triangle shirtwaist factory
on the corner
of Washington Place and Greene Street
in New York City, March 25th, 1911:
Ardito, Bassino, Benanti, Billota, Brunetti,
Cammarata, Caputo, Carlisi, Caruso, Ciminello,
Cirrito, Colletti, Cordiano, Del Castillo,
Floresta, Franco, Giannattasio, Grasso,

Tortorelli-Lauletti, L'Abbate, Leone,
Maiale, Maiale, Maltese, Maltese, Maltese,
Manaria, Midolo, Nicolosi,
Panno, Pasqualicchio, Pinelli, Prato, Prestifilippo, Salemi,
Saracino, Saracino, Stellino, Terranova, Tortorelli, Uzzo, Viviano,
and one Jamaican: Daisy Lopez Fitze whose Barese grandniece
Fortuna writes of her memory.
Two elevator operators
who saved a hundred and fifty as they burned:
Giuseppe Zito, Gaspare Mortillaro.
Four war veterans who delivered ice in the Bronx:
Giuseppe Rocco Lanzillotto, Carmine Lanzillotto,
Saverio Lanzillotto, Mikey Piccinnini,
One civilian iceman Giuseppe Petruzzelli.
One self-flagellating preacher, Savonarola
One astronomer, Bruno,
One oh really yes philosopher, Aurelius,
Two painters, one who painted a man mooning the Sistine Chapel:
Michelangelo Buonarroti, and one who told us dark from light:
Michelangelo Merisi da Caravaggio.
One poet who took us to hell and purgatory
and heaven, Dante Alighieri,
One actor whose *faccia* shows the suffering and passion of all of us:
Nannarella: Anna Magnani, La Magnani.
One director who knew closing one's eyes
is where visions come from: Federico Fellini,
One composer who saved my mother by opening her lungs:
Giacomo Puccini,
A legion of poets, martyrs,
saints: including one rich man's son who listened
to the musings of sparrows Francesco di Bernadone,
partigiani, sculptors, painters
and women who lived into their old age
alone.

PART II

Your Eye You Keep on the Ball

Michael Jackson Saint of Taking Off All Masks

Hail Michael!
Full of Music One Glove of Grace
Saint of Taking Off All Masks!
Mask of Gender
Mask of Race
Mask of Age
Mask of Sexuality
Mask of Normalcy
And finally
Mask of Life
Release us from prescription overdosing.
Rip us from skin identities
that we may live deeper
in the regions of the heart leagues
from the epidermis.
Blessed Art Thou Amongst Performance Artists
And Blessed is the Fruit of Thy Agony

Holy Michael!
Dancer of God
Remover of All Pigment From Skin
In an age when to darken skin is the multi-billion dollar industry
of profiteer whites
Heavenly Michael! Eternal Moonwalk
Standing in wind beyond whiteface and blackface
Who Sang "I'm not gonna spend my life being a color"
Who Beat It to Jingoes
Heal us all with the fire of your artistry,
Your spontaneous combustion.
Pray for Us Masked Souls
That our spirits may move about our body
Like flame to wick, Amen
Can You Feel It, The Way You Make Me Feel, Off The Wall,
Why does he do it that way, tell them that it's human nature
Bless us Freaks in all our nature
that we may devour our own shadow

devour projections of cute and become Bad and Dangerous
Release us from the trappings of normalcy
That we may shout oh so loud, Rock With You,
Calibrate our souls, I'll Be There
Pray in the persecution of the crowd,
we may Unmask! Unmask! Unmask!
1,2,3 Easy As ABC
Amen

Lunch Break
Lenox Avenue and 135th Street

"This ain't right. This ain't right,"
Cody stood six four in velour,
Shook his head over her corpse,
"She saved my life. I'm telling you.
This ain't right. We out there runnin the streets.
We out there causing crossfire. And she go down?
Uh-huh. Uh-huh. This ain't right.
I got shot and brought to Harlem Hospital.
Pamela was there, working the O.R.
I thanked God she was my nurse.
She looked at me and said,
"Cody!? Uh-huh! You ain't dying on me! You hear!"
Five days later I woke up. Pamela was there, standing over me.
Now she's here like this? Uh-huh.
Here we got our own ways of dealing with things.
Here we got our own laws.
You ever need something, you call me."

Pink balloons and streamers filled the church hall.
Platters of chicken and cole slaw waited under tin foil.
This was supposed to be her fiftieth birthday party.
Cousins flew up, presents wrapped,
their Carolina drawls curled up in Harlem,
tickled necks, made heads tilt.
Blue and purple gels covered the lights over the church altar,
Diagonal beams highlighted her head and feet,
In red velvet seats at the wake, cousins threw their heads back.
Her only son was nowhere to be found.
A roll of paper towels was passed around
to absorb the grief and murmurs,
"I just hope he didn't go off looking for the man who killed her."

After the van slammed her up into the air,
Pamela's body was carried back to her co-workers
at Harlem Hospital.

She was on her lunch break
when she crossed Lenox Avenue between two parked cars.

the asphalt held traces of her
broken glass
and stains.

Girl Picking Daffodils
Central Park, 72nd Street off Central Park West

It is yours as all the earth is, Pick
You are entitled to it, Pick it
You are living,
The wind is within you calling
Pick it to receive it
Pick it you love it
Walk by you love it even more
Walk by let it live
Do not pick
It belongs to no one.

Trample it. Earths recover.
Death is a glorious
god the destroyer
of all things
Return.
Pick it you are it
Pick it to die
Walk by and remember it to a stranger in your glance
Run by it and remember what it is in passing.

Pick it you cannot
Once you pick it is gone
It will die
Take it to water then
Celebrate its decay
Be while it wilts
Wait with it
Pick it to relieve it
Pick it put it elsewhere
Hold it till it is no more
Hold it like a stick of faith the poor do
Like the rich do riches
This is mine
Wine fear and bread,

Girl, pick
and trample that flower bed then!
Pick!
Let someone see you
Pick!
Knowing you can never make anything so beautiful.

How to Approach a Basketball Court
Zerega Avenue, Bronx

With or without a ball you enter the court.
Someone else always has a ball.
You don't have to bring your own.
You come, you play.
You come, you forget.
You step onto the court. You rebound the ball.
If it went in, you pass it back to the shooter.
If it missed, you shoot it yourself.
This is how to approach a basketball court.
Everyone looks at the hoop.
It is you who released the ball but no one looks at you.
They look at the hoop.
They get to know you by the spin you put on the ball,
By the arc, the throw, by how it enters the hoop.
There is no net. There is no need for a net.
We are here because it is essential.
The ball is the only thing constant.
This practice.
This bouncing.
This life.

How to Catch a Fly Ball in Oncoming Traffic

Saint Raymond's Avenue and Zerega Avenue, Bronx

With a car coming at you, you face the open sky.
You never miss a pop fly because a car is coming at you.
You listen. You turn your ear to the horizon.
The ball is in the air.
Your feet are moving beneath you.
Your ear tracks the speed the car is coming at you.
Your eye you keep on the ball.
You know a car is coming without needing to look.
You don't want to stop the car,
just like you don't want the car to stop the play.
With your throwing arm you flag the car around you.
You know which side of the street the ball is favoring in the wind.
You wave the car to the other side of you.
You can temporarily halt the car
'til the ball is square in your hands.
The car inches forward 'til you got it, then the car proceeds.
The car is your audience rushing to find you.
The car came all this way,
down this particular street, around several corners, jumped
the exit ramp to back up 'round the corner to see
you make this play.
The car in the middle of the play is part of the play.
It's all in the timing.

What Country Do You Live In?
Hughes Avenue and 187th Street, Bronx

My block is my world.
Light blue sky bends
around the deep blue mailbox on the corner.
I hoist myself up like mounting a horse.
From here I sit and watch the world.
The rush of blacktop up against the lip of the corner.

I remember the bore tide at Turnagain Arm, in Anchorage.
I sat high on the rocks at Beluga Point and watched for hours,
as a six foot wall of water roared in from the sea
loud as Hells Angels, the river changed direction before my eyes.

Imagine you're running away
and the street drags you back home again?
Full moon, the molten magnetic iron core of the earth,
big as the moon,
collaborate to push you back inland to your private calanque,
a place no one has seen. "It used to be a grotto," you say,
look at my drawings on the cave walls.
But all they see is an impasse, a crag in the rock, and on their faces,
the oppression of concern.

American Cars
Christopher Street

After the eviction I sat under a blanket
in a sword of sunlight, listened to seagulls by the Hudson River
behind the wheel of my Dodge Spirit, read newspapers,
A guy got seven parking tickets before the police noticed
he was dead in the backseat of his BMW.
A BMW with a small backseat.
The papers say he has no kids.
The papers say he wasn't happy.
His neighbors say he was the most intelligent man they ever knew.
A real intellectual, with back pain.

I think I'll outlive my Dodge Spirit.
American cars are better than foreign cars for some things.
Plush backseats with springs, full bench front seats.
Room to lay out in.
Cheap as pine coffins.

The Doctor's Touch
68th Street and York Avenue

Warm the stethoscope in your hands.
Listen to the heart.
Feel for it, in the neck, armpits, and with your eyes
fixed on the ceiling, one by one,
breasts. Find it, hiding beneath the clavicle.
Pull it up like a plum from
below the bone. Under the jaw, there,
find it twice.
Roll it between your fingers.
Say, "It's a good sign if this hurts."
Now with your eyes on the floor, push
into the crevices of the groin.
The hiding gets harder now.
Under the ribs and ask
for a deeper breath.
Ask if this hurts.
Run your hands over every pore of the skin for lumps,
for something not quite right,
for a sudden deep deep valley.
Press the abdomen.
Name the liver when you find it.
Press on.
Name the kidneys.

I am tired and know not why.
I take in two sips of breath.
I say nothing.
You press on.
Name
My spleen.

Strike One
New Jersey

My first cancer I got diagnosed at Seaside Heights
by a boardwalk portrait artist named Rhoda Shapiro.
It was the summer before I left for college,
the last day of a two week stay with my pitcher's
family in their bungalow on the Jersey shore.
A pitcher and catcher are a duo
who spend as much time together off-season as possible throwing
strikes, curves, knuckleballs, pitch-outs, sinkers,
refining signals, the catcher pops up out of a squat
throws down to second to nab the steal,
makes the play at the plate, swipes a caught ball
at imaginary runners sliding home.
For two weeks I caught two hundred throws twice a day,
seventy-five warm-up and down, the balance slung hard,
two hundred pop-squats barefoot in the sand.
Each day turned me a bit more blonde, fit and tan,
ready to jump into action
at Brown, where I was a softball recruit for the varsity team.

I wanted to get my mother a great present not crap,
not a silk-screened Elvis mirror, not an air-brushed
t-shirt of some palm tree paradise,
not one of the minions of stuffed ETs prevalent that summer,
no, more of a forever keepsake,
something she could remember me by, something
to represent this point in time.
College would change everything.
I'd never come back home.

I took one last walk alone,
to the batting range,
slugged the ball back into the net, line drives up the middle,
my hands rang from the shock of the aluminum bat
against the softball's heart.
I walked down the boardwalk one last time

passed the portrait artists who shouted at me day after day,
flashed drawings of Marilyn Monroe and John Travolta,
said it wouldn't take long.
No one in my family ever had a portrait done before.
I was going off to the Ivy League,
the Ivy League was all about portraits in stately rooms,
My mother would love it!
I directed my steps toward one of the artists.
She wore a big sun hat,
a Bella Abzug hat that created a yellow arena around her head.
We agreed on fifty bucks, all I had in my pocket.
"Plenty of detail for fifty bucks," she guaranteed me,
"not a pen line caricature."
Her name was Rhoda Shapiro.

I couldn't see her hand as it drew,
her arms moved at a rapid speed, automatic
as the pitching machine in the batting cage.
She asked me questions about my life
She chose reds and yellows from her case of pastels,
Her eyes landed on different parts of me.
When she was decidedly finished, she wished me good luck with
my future,
and turned the drawing toward me.

Rhoda had drawn a girl a little more feminine and gorgeous,
fuller lipped, feathered hair a little blonder than my own,
eyes a deeper blue,
and a glow, a white thin halo surrounding the whole bust.
My pitcher laughed back at the bungalow,
said it looked nothing like me
but I could see the resemblance.
It was a culturally idealized version of me, some iconic combination
of the Mona Lisa magnetism of John Travolta drawing you in,
and the full bursting lipped ripe beauty of Marilyn Monroe
enticing you to take a bite,
and that's just what this point in my life was all about, certainly
my college application essays and recommendations were

as blonde, blue-eyed, with as exaggerated and energetic
a virgin's glow.

When I got home, I handed the scroll to my mother magisterially
telling her how I would miss her now that I was moving on.
She unrolled the portrait and said,
"What's this lump on your neck?" immediately turning
her attention from the portrait to my neck,
where her hand landed on what Rhoda Shapiro had drawn
and only my mother saw, a bulge
on the right side of my neck,
Rhoda had outlined in red and yellow
a diagnosis, a misshapen neck, a lump like a stop sign
amidst a blonde waterfall.
As it turned out, Rhoda's eye had the accuracy of a sonogram.

"How'd your mother like the portrait?" my pitcher asked.
"She didn't really say," I said, "she took one look
and said she's sending me straightaway to the doctor tomorrow.
Something about a biopsy. Maybe I should have gotten her the
Elvis mirror?"

Strike Two
Sag Harbor, New York

My second cancer
I got diagnosed by a surrealist painter named Ulek Tosher.
He sat in a wheelchair on the main drag next to the bus stop.
I crossed the street to get an ice-cream cone.
The thought came to me: get that old man a cone too. Vanilla.
I walked directly for him, handed him the cone.
His face lit up and he invited me up to his apartment
to see his paintings.
Up a flight of stairs, his Jamaican aide went ahead
to open the door.
I stepped into a room filled with Chagall-like paintings.
Fish flying with onions. Bull's horns. Tall onions.
Rococo wrought iron fences over garbage pails.
Swirls of blues, greens, orange, black and white fish.
I was amazed at the magnificence of Ulek's canvasses.

He began to write me letters. I became a muse.
He mailed me a photo of a painting he did of me,
"Portrait With You In Mind."
He recognized my soul deeper than the features on my face,
crooked blues eyes of two different sizes
an anoxic hue, a blue head,
Sleeping at the base of the neck,
a man curled up around a light bulb.
The painting perplexed me, until my neck began to grow.
I went to doctors.
Five needle biopsies came back "negative."
Everyone was inconclusive, except Ulek,
The man was asleep around the lightbulb.

I went to a sixth doctor. He was old school.
No insurance. No credit cards.
Blue and brown glass bottles, cures and tinctures of a bygone era.
Five hundred in cash. He examined me head to toe,
then joined the ranks of the inconclusive.

I walked out to the waiting room, handed over all my cash,
shoved my arm through my snorkel jacket sleeve
and opened the door to leave.
The doctor stepped in and shouted off the cuff,
"If it keeps growing, I'd get it the hell outta there."
Those words rang in my head as I walked up First Avenue,
"Get it the hell outta there,"
"Get it the hell outta there."
I telephoned Sloan-Kettering from the sidewalk.
Scheduled with the surgeon who wore Ferragamo shoes.

The thyroid was asleep,
packed with cancer.
They took the whole thing.
"Even the isthmus," the surgeon told me.
Even the isthmus I repeated in my head.
Even the isthmus I never knew I had.
Ulek saw all.
The man asleep around a lightbulb.

Nights Like This
Election Night 2009, 125th Street & Adam Clayton Powell Boulevard

(sing)
Nights like this I wonder what my father'd say.
Nights like this I wonder,
Nights like this I wonder,
Nights like this I wonder what my father'd say.

I must remake my mind.
I must remake it.
I must remake it.
I must remake my mind.

I think that's why I gotta die.
I think that's why I gotta die.
Cause there's only so much I can change my mind in one lifetime,
I think that's why I gotta die.

So a new mind can find its way.
A new mind can find it,
A new mind can find it,
A new mind can find its way.

Daddy your world is worlds away.
Daddy your world is worlds away.
Where ice picks settled scores and hatred burned as fuel
in foxholes, alleyways, kitchens, and boiler rooms.
I wonder what you'd say today's Election Day.

(recite)
Election Day morning I sat in a diner in Yonkers with my mother.
We sat next to a wall that was all mirrors.
I saw the head of an old man with a twisted red face.
He talked loud enough over his breakfast
for the whole diner to hear what he had to say.
The back of his wife's head nodded as if she was just glad to be fed.
He chewed and looked around,

"The Jews won't let a Socialist Muslim be elected."
I swallowed. Disgust. Rye toast.
Coffee with milk. Silence. Scrambled eggs. Fear
of what wanted to come out of my mouth and spue over everyone.
I took small bites and sips, buttered my toast, read the newspaper,
looked in the mirror wall.

We voted, my mother and I, in silent booths where I felt free
away from mens' voices around tables, and complicit
chewing women.
I must remake my mind.
I must trust the miles of my guts
to digest everything and get rid of it.
Silent. Invisible. Confessional.
I pulled the lever.
The curtain closed behind me.
I faced the wall of names and flipped the Democrat switches.
I flipped No on the proposals I sped read to understand
but the key words did not give me the intentions I needed to
capeesh.
I jiggled the toggles up and down just to make sure
they stayed down
when my forefinger left them they didn't jump back up.
So easy. Easier than a light switch.
That's it?
Millions of us, turning off the light.
Morte la luce.
The hhhhtttttddt of the lever as I pulled to finalize my vote
hhhhttttddddt
decision time.
cockpit.
Let's fly, America. Let's fly now.
Lever like a rudder,
Pull back into the sky
Raise the nose of this baby
Ameriga: named after a nice Italian boy.
o-ba-MAH o-ba-MAH o-ba-MAH
It's a short runway

But long enough
Barack is beautiful !
Ba-Rock is beautiful !
Djembe beats
We're gonna clear the mountains just ahead
Pull up out of this valley
Djembe beats
Heart paddles
Defibrillator for the world baby.
Djembe beats
Every heart back
Harlem cheers dancing in the street.
Kenya picks the goat for slaughter.

Tonight is the night all will be compared to.

At eleven o'clock p.m.,
I can't resist the tug any longer
to be with New Yorkers in the streets
Peel up off the couch
Zip up my dungarees
Walk out of the silent Yonkers night
A night I can't find the moon
The blinds tucked tight in dim windows.

I drive down the West Side Highway listening to the radio
a white news reporter struggles for metaphors
To compare this night in Harlem,
"It's like your home team won. It's like the World Series. It's like
the Yankees." "No," he scrambled, "It's like the Yankees
and the Knicks and the Mets and the Rangers and every other team
all won at once."
I shut the radio off.

Tonight is the night all will be compared to.
I park the car on 125th Street and walk east.
125th and Adam Clayton Powell Boulevard
A man runs in circles carrying a giant American flag.

The bus stops in the middle of 125th
and the bus driver takes photos.
Hugs. High-fives out the windows of the bus.
Camera crews. No ones a stranger.
A store named LAZARUS in bright letters
each letter a different color
as if the whole damn country was just raised from the dead.

The Apollo's marquee is bold and simple:
President Barack Obama.
Djembe brings the dance out of kneecaps up spines out shoulder
rotator cuffs rotating
Harlem like Capetown.
Harlem Capetown
Djembe Free at Last Supper Skip the Supper
in circles at intersections of the greatest minds of all generations
Suffering shamans coming to a head
busting open like moons in African dresses with Yes We Can
t-shirts pulled over big breasts
we are the people - that have seen one another at protests
we are the people - in welfare lines
we are the people - who've never danced in the streets all together
"It's about time!" the bouncer outside The Lenox Lounge yells.
The lines are long,
I walk up to Sylvia's for a drink.
A woman sells President Obama t-shirts
out of a pushcart on the corner.
I get one. When I was a kid I had a Mickey Mouse for President
t-shirt with Richard Nixon's hands widespread with peace signs.
What are Barack's signifying hands?
I could hear a voice coaching him
before he walks out onto the stage at Grant Park,
"Whatever you do, do not raise your fist in the air."

There is an ice sculpture outside Sylvia's.
A block of ice for each letter: O B A M A
Ice on an altar with balloons in red white and blue spirals.
Italians no doubt sculpted it.

You don't get that clear ice just anywhere.
I know that ice.
I know the clarity of it, the chiseled face of that ice.
I touched the texture of the ice.
I know exactly where you get that ice.
The ice house used to be on 110th Street,
but they got priced out
and now make ice on Bathgate Avenue in the Bronx.
where the ice continually moves so it freezes from the inside out.
I held my cell phone out in front of me
and took a photo with the letter A.
I touch the ice and think of my father.
They don't deliver block ice much anymore
except for sculptures, it's hard to get a block of ice,
men don't want to carry it up steps anymore.
I stood in the red light, my palm on the ice of the letter A in
OBAMA.

I must remake my mind.
Why aren't we like this all the time,
a man named Bernie said hugging me.
I see everyone differently today, Audrey said over the phone.
Nights like this I wonder what my father'd say.
I touch the ice.

(sing)
I must remake my mind.
I must remake it.
I must remake it.
I must remake my mind.

One day I gotta die.
One day I gotta die.
For there's only so much I can change one mind in one lifetime.
I think that's why I gotta die.

Nights like this I wonder what my father'd say.
Nights like this I wonder,

Nights like this I wonder,
Nights like this I wonder what my father'd say.

I must remake my mind.
I must remake it.
I must remake it.
I must remake my mind.

I think that's why I gotta die.
I think that's why I gotta die.
Cause there's only so much I can change my mind in one lifetime,
I think that's why I gotta die.

So a new mind can find its way.
A new mind can find it,
A new mind can find it,
A new mind can find its way.

Daddy your world is worlds away.
Daddy your world is worlds away.
Where ice picks settled scores and hatred burned as fuel
in foxholes, alleyways, kitchens, and boiler rooms.
I wonder what you'd say today's Election Day.

Licking Batteries

and feeling the undersides of wine bottles
is how I got my lesbian training.
For this, I gotta thank the tough guys in my family.

When I was four, my father gave me a bucket of batteries.
Told me to separate out the dead ones from the live.
We were in the basement. I turned to look for a radio.
"Get back here," he said, "you gotta lick 'em.
Focus the tip of your tongue on the cathode.
It'll sting if there's a charge.
The Sodium Ion goes through the receptor in the tongue."
I licked my first battery with a flat open tongue
like an ice-cream cone,
'til my father showed me how to focus the tip,
and taste the salty volts.
A charge was salty and stung the tongue.
I became expert. I could divide a bucket of batteries in no time.
I didn't realize the practical application of this skill
until I was twenty-one
and tasted my lover's clitoris. I sharpened my tongue to a small tip
and lured her clitoris out of its hood.
The clitoris has a pulse, a charge coursing through it.
If volts shoot through me I know,
This one's live.
Volts I can taste.

When I was seven my uncle taught me
how to pick out a good bottle of wine.
Bottles my uncle handed me, bottles of what he called good *vino*.
"Feel the bottom of it," he told me. With my three middle fingers
I feel the smooth concavity up to the knuckles.
My uncle smiled, threw his head back and let out a big, "Ahhh Haaa!"
That's how you tell a good wine.
I didn't realize the practical application of this skill
until I was twenty-one
and entering a smooth open cunt.

I Breathed in the Twin Towers

I lived on a hill in Brooklyn,
my table pushed next to the windows, overlooked lower Manhattan.
Two steeples cut tall triangles out of the sky,
the First Dutch Reform Church and Saint Francis' Church.
Out over the roof of Key Food, the Statue of Liberty,
a tiny lit green candle on the far end of my table.

The Twin Towers bounced the setting sun into my room,
drenched the room in an umber glow.
Sunset. Ancient round pink disc descent,
through the table saw horizon.
Two rectangular digitized strips of blazing gold and pink,
the eastern faces of the Towers, beamed sun at my
disco ball hung in the window
fragmenting sunlight into a galaxy
of spinning glittering sun shards.

My bed was in the far corner of the room.
One night while I slept, breathing deeply,
Tower One whirled up into the air, a helix through the sky,
through my window, right up in through my left nostril,
all the floors piled up, one back on top of one another
in my left lung.
Then Tower Two took off, whirling,
a slinky of itself, up through the night sky,
in through my window, into my right nostril,
where it stacked up again, floor by floor and stood tall
in my right lung.

I thought it was a dream.
But when my Pulmonologist at Sloan-Kettering took a CAT-Scan,
she saw a shadow on my lung, called me in to the X-ray Suite.
"I don't know what it is," she pointed at a tiny white shadow
which clung to the lining of my left lung.
"Let's keep our eye on it. It could be the Twin Towers.
I want to repeat the test in two months."

Root Canal at Ground Zero

Me and the city
drilled to the root.
I look out Dr. Neidle's window
down into the big gaping hole
and feel the city in my jaw bone
down to the schist.

Anxiety at Sunset

I know I'm a Nooyawkah because I get anxiety at sunset
if I'm somewhere there ain't a bodega or coffee shop
I can run to any time of night.

I know I'm a Nooyawkah because I get anxiety in the country
where I can't go out in a thunderstorm and see some babe
casually roller skating by in a bikini slinkin' jumps
on wet asphalt 'cross the black tarmac of Houston Street.

I know I'm a Nooyawkah cause if I'm outta town too long
I have to come back
before I forget how to think straight,
walk the blocks by which to measure my soul.
Blocks like pages turn.

I know I'm a Nooyawkah cause my accent is a relic
that hits you like an open smack.
Cause I was born here.
You can hear it in me rrright?
You can hear the Dutchified good Bronx tones?
The Bronx was Dutch man.
We still got the guttural tones. Here it is. This is it.
I'm a relic. I ain't Dutch. You know me. Am I Dutch?

I know I'm a Nooyawkah cause anyone with a good job
ran from this accent.
I know I'm a Nooyawkah cause I breathe best in exhaust.
I know I'm a Nooyawkah cause if I'm sneezing upstate
alls I gotta do is breathe
over a bucket of hot tar.
I know I'm a Nooyawkah cause I don't give a ffffhuck.
I know I'm a Nooyawkah.
I see sewer caps as gorgeous pizzelle irons.
I crave the competing smells the streets, ravioli vindaloo chow mein
sancocho in little Bogota around the corner from Masala
in Little Bombay.

I down vino in Tribeca on a candlelit loading dock
as cars descend into the tunnel swallow to Jersey.

I know I'm a Nooyawkah.
I walk river to river, river to bay,
I see five major bridges in one day,
the most beautiful named after a *paesan*.

I know I'm a Nooyawkah with neon blood,
radioactive spit: Keep Back Two Hundred Feet.
I feel solo in a minyan,
transcendent in a chicken wire rooftop pigeon coop.
A three and a half fingered butcher will sing at my funeral.

I know I'm a Nooyawkah
cause I move with sudden turns and spirals,
spaldeen ascensions over city streets,
down concrete pathways,
I love how fences smell in the rain
and curbside gush to the sewergrates.
My voice echoes in tight Bronx alleys.
My bacteria is from Mars,
where oceans grow upward from frozen ground water.
I divine water over corner sewergrates,
where I hear the underground babble all the way
from the *acquedotto* offa *Via Appia*.

I know I'm a Nooyawkah cause I'm not Dutch
but I sound sound Dutch.
I know I'm a Nooyawkah cause I never evicted
the First Peoples out of the Land Where The Sun Was Born,
I know I'm a Nooyawkah 'cause I can walk on a diagonal
from Saint Mark's to Times Square.
All on a diagonal.
I know I'm a Nooyawkah cause I get close as I can to speeding cars
and run my finger along their sides to prove them of their dust.
I know I'm a Nooyawkah. My chemo I take to go.
A license for hypodermics is in my back pocket.

Sub-Q, I.M., I.V., Port, I cross the blood brain barrier. I do it all.
I know Sweet Sixteens don't always come before funerals.
I know my sun doesn't set behind New Jersey.
I know I am an American.
Born on the mainland, The Bronx,
but it is on schist I stand.
I remove all surface topography, superficialities,
get down to crack ourselves open to bedrock and build from there.
I know I am a Nooyawkah because on schist I stand.
I know I'm a Nooyawkah because it is to be
with Nooyawkahs that I put up with all this.

Bucket of Tar

The men are outside tarring the street.
They carry buckets of fire.
Tar burning black.
They burn it, pour it, roll it.
Men in orange shirts.
Tar doesn't breed bugs or need bugs
like God's grass green.
Flat black. Hot cover. This earth.
No creature may crawl inside here.
This black muck stops each cell of the breathing earth.
The skin of the earth breathes no longer.
And do I?

My mother told me, "Tar layers never get colds."
She held my hand and walked me to where they worked,
instructed me to breathe. "Burning tar is good," she said,
"for your tight angel wings and lungs."

When I was four I stepped into a bucket of tar in the sun,
I liked to stick my feet into things to test their depths:
puddles, sand barrels, fresh cement, cans of thick paint.
A bucket of tar was too good to pass up.
Warm tar slithered up to my waist.
I tried to lift one leg. I held onto the sides of the bucket and pulled.
It took a moment for me to realize I was stuck,
in our backyard, in a bucket of tar alone in the sun.
A fat man, tarred and feathered, paraded
down the street in my mind,
feathers mocked his entrapment.

My wings have no power. I cried
a long loud red hot scream.
The squeak of the gate.
My father appears laughing, "Whatchyou doin' in there!"
He pulls me up. The bucket clings.
He kicks the bucket away from me.

The tar takes my sneakers whole, my feet are released.
The screen door slams three times before it shuts.
My mother runs down the back steps,
They stripped me. She called for turpentine and a brush,
cursed and bagged my clothes.
These were people who never threw anything away.

My angel wings are clipped.
I cannot lift myself up off the ground.
I need two mirrors just to see the stubs on my back,
wing bones push skin,
like a chick breaks the egg shell.
Still I remember how to fly.

Red Sky

Did
you
see
her
eye
red
sky?
Did
you
see
sky
red
eye?
Sad
run.
Did
you
see
sun?
Her
sun?
Did
you
see
the
red
sun
cry
red
sky?
Did
you
sky
red
eye?
Cry red sky.

Alone

Your absence in waves
ascends my heart,
rung by fateful rung.
Your name has climbed the bell tower.

Where must I go
at what hour
to hear your name called through the streets
by any voice but my own?

PART III

**All Will Be Forgotten
'Cept This Gold Light We Made Together**

The Queer Kiss at the Altar

Dearly Beloved,
Take occasion to kiss.
There are many kisses in life.
Our Mother's Kiss
Kiss of Liberation
Puppy Dog Kiss
Kiss of Revolution
The Dangerous Public Display of Affection
Cheek Kiss of Friendship
Forehead Kiss of Adoration
Double Cheek Kiss
Triple Cheek Kiss
Mwah mwah Air Kiss
Kiss of Leaving
Kiss to Raise the Dead
The Kiss of Coming Home
Kiss to Bury the Dead
I don't know if I'll ever see you again Kiss
I know I'll never see you again Kiss
Kiss Your Hand in Respect
The Kiss to End All Kisses
Blow a Kiss
Spin the Bottle Kiss
Kiss to Meet Your Father for the First Time Kiss
Kiss to Awaken Sleeping Beauty
Prison Visit Kiss
First Kiss
First Gay Kiss when the world stops and your gut drops
The Imagined Kiss
The Remembered Kiss
The Kiss You Can't Forget
The Kiss You Hope For
The No Turning Back Kiss
In the Act-Up days, before roadblocks
and corporate sponsored floats,
before we were a voting block, a lobby, a market,

we stopped traffic for our marches,
not with bullhorns or orange vests,
but with a kiss. The Kiss To Stop Traffic.
Cars honking, we paired up in the crosswalks,
held each other, breathed deep and dove into a kiss.
If we did this alone back then we'd get spit on and cursed or worse.
So we did it together.
The Kiss-In Kiss
The Queer Kiss At The Altar is
The Kiss That Insists
We Kiss For The Chance To Be Ordinary
We've been cursed shunned outlawed locked-up beat-up
medicated tolerated accepted celebrated
Seal with a kiss today what governments will seal tomorrow
by edict.
You may
now
kiss.

E Shred
Babylon, New York

Penny a pound for steel frame.
PVC vinyl. Two cents a pound.
Wires. Boards. Drives. Chips.
Plastics. Contaminates. Tungsten. Gold.
A computer comes from 8 countries, or so I been told.

We all thought Daddy was crazy,
rippin' apart computers into coffee cans.
But he was the industry of the future,
with his worn tools, bent thoughts, bare hands.

The man was just doing what needed to be done.
E Shred! E Shred!
The man was just doing what needed to be done.
E Shred! E Shred!

Maps of Okinawa over his lap, fifty years past VJ Day.
Lanzi saw how the Japanese defense coulda kept him
and the Marines away.
In the 1990's computers appeared in sidewalk trash,
Lanzi took 'em to the mental home.
Stripped 'em apart with his bare hands,
on his workbench bone by bone.
Ten years he filled hundreds of jars with the metals
he extracted with precision,
Lined the basement walls jar by jar, that was his decision.

The man was just doing what needed to be done!
E Shred! E Shred!
The man was just doing what needed to be done!
E Shred! E Shred!

Gotta destroy all this information.
Gotta destroy now!

Gotta destroy all this information.
Gotta destroy now!

For a few hours I'd take my father out, for a walk by the bay.
We'd stare into the Atlantic
and hear what the fishermen had to say.
Over the ocean we stared off east, fantasized about Italy,
talked of our cousins over there and dreamt of what life might be.

For all the years I knew my father, he gambled at the track,
never took "No" for answer, drank his coffee black.
He handed me a can of stripped copper wire and a vial of gold
filaments as parting gifts,
I sat by him in his hospital bed, let the silence mend all our rifts.
Daddy's last wish was to be buried in the VA cemetery,
in the earth we put him to bed.
Not long after I read an article about the newest industry called,
"E-Shred."
Millions of dollars were being made, taking old computers apart,
shredding component parts and information.
Separating precious metals, contaminate waste and components,
clear across the nation.

Penny a pound for steel frame. PVC vinyl, 2 cents a pound.
Wires. Boards. Drives. Chips.
Insulated copper, 20 cents a pound
cast aluminum frame, 30 cents a pound
metals, plastics, contaminates, cast aluminum base
hunks of copper, steel plated magnetic disc
diamonds in the rough,
bare copper wire, ninety cents for dirty, a dollar for clean
nickel coated aluminum disks, 25 cents a pound
aluminum clips, 35 cents a pound
motor disks, hard drive disks, aluminum, stainless, and steel
irony aluminum, breakage, 7 cents a pound, network drive cards,
soundcards, CPU chip, aluminum heat sink, battery,
memory cards,
IC chips, small aluminum heatsinks by torroid inductors

copper wound inductors, ferrite, ten cents a pound
male female connectors, gold plated pins
tantalum capacitors, motherboard, 50 cents a pound
network and drive cards, gold fingers and IC chips
copper wound torroid inductor, cpu/sim chips
flat backed grey pentiums with gold pins and square
76% Tungsten, two to four dollars
ceramic chips, aluminum plate and grid
square of gold pins, cyrix chips: silicone with gold pins
Copper. Silver. Platinum. Gold.

I wish I didn't think Daddy was crazy,
with his bare hands, worn tools, and hours all alone
next to the furnace.
The man was just doing what needed to be done.

Front Line Flesh

Nobody ever expected us to walk away.
We was front line flesh. Cannon fodder.
Placed to take bullets the sky refused.
Bullets go right through this Soft Great Wall.
I thought they was kidding, mapping my body out in boot camp,
birthmarks, making notes, marking down the trails of scars
the Bronx streets and the backside of Papa's open hand made.
This mole. That scar. Whole constellations of beauty marks.
I was green. A real wiseguy.
I said, "What's the Marines writing a book about me?"
"No, soldier," the Sarge said, looking me up and down,
"that's so we can name what's left
after Japfire blows your dogtags to bits."
Come home in one piece? Fagetaboutit.
I stamped my name and serial number
all over myself in sections
so they won't make no mistake.
I swore, no military guesswork.
Mamma ain't getting nobody's parts
but my own.

Blue Pill

Attendant came 'round with a shot of tap water and a blue pill.
Watched Daddy swallow, turned and walked away,
I can see her still.
Daddy spun round spit into his hand, walked two flights down,
to the basement mental home boiler room.
Blue pill. Blue pill. Blue pill. Red white and blue.

Fifty years the wars been over.
"Goodbye and good luck," eye to eye, he told her,
"we fought for peace, I got no peace still."
Gimme another blue pill.
In the basement mental home boiler room.
Blue pill. Blue pill. Blue pill. Red white and blue.

Did they ever tell you you were so ill,
You had to take the Blue Pill?
Did they ever tell you you were so ill,
You had to take the Blue Pill?

A war veteran diagnosed for all his ills.
A pocket full of blue pills.
Alone in the basement, safe from landmines,
Taking apart computers, stripping time.
In the basement mental home boiler room.
Blue pill. Blue pill. Blue pill. Red white and blue.

How to Wake Up a Marine in a Foxhole

Asleep, my father was a landmine indiscriminate,
It was my detail to wake him.
You want him to see you.
You want him to know it's you.
If you nudge him awake he might think you're the enemy. No!
You take the thumb. Listen to me.
You press under the middle of the eyebrow.
You let some light seep into the eye.
You press 'til you see some of the white of that eye.
Light, gradual light is the gentlest way of waking up.
Makes sense, right?
That's why they got that sun there over the horizon.
You peel the thumb back gently, carefully
As if not wanting to smear a thumbprint left behind
on the skin of the eyelid.
You wait to make sure the eye will hold open.
The eye you touch opens first, then both,
not a breath between them.
You want him to see you.
You want him to know
What he sees doesn't register with what's in his head.
Everything has led up to this.
Everything happens because of it.
You snatch the dream away from him.
It all occurs in the cleft of a second.
Boom! The eye opens.
He's awake!
Without being startled!
Without jumping awake ready to kill!
He sees you.
He knows it's you. And he trusts you
by the greens in your helmet and the shape of your eyes
and he's awake.
He knows
it's you.

Stray Kamikaze

The sky was a dirty grey.
The guy next to me says, "Hey Lanzi, it's gonna rain."
I say, "That ain't no rain."
We was three hundred miles from Hiroshima.
It was August. Around your brother's birthday.
Next couple of days there's some rumor going around, saying
the U.S. had dropped the *adam* bomb.
With one bomb, wiped out a whole city.
Of course, we didn't believe it.
How can you level a city with one bomb?
Bombs we was used to blew holes big as houses,
big as this house maybe.
But a whole city? How could that be?
We figured it musta been a rumor the U.S. was spreading
to make 'em stop fighting before we used the *adam* bomb.
But Japanese surrender?
That's a whaddyacall,
Whaddyacall when two things just don't go together?
Right. That's the word. That's what that was.
You see, to a Japanese soldier, surrender was disgrace.
Against his honor. And the way them Japanese believed,
how you died, mattered to your soul.
To die in battle was the best your soul could do.

Then they said the war was over and they showed us lots of movies.
The guys would sit around outside the barracks on benches
and you know, watch the movies.
I never watched the movies.
There's always a stray Kamikaze
to come right down on you
with a machine gun.

How to Dig a Foxhole

Same time we was digging the front line
through a fresh layer of dead earth.
Didn't take our boots off for tree weeks
then we traded socks and moved on.
On the front, you had to dig a foxhole. You had no choice.
If it rained, you sat in mud all night.
And it always rained.
You take this here entrenching shovel.
You dig in, right through the bones of the earth.
You dig.
    "Ooooof! Can't dig in here, Sir. Dead here, Sir."
    "Perimeter zone established.
    Two to a foxhole. Every five feet. Dig in Private!"
You dig. Who knows what you come up with.
Maggots. A hand. A set of ribs.
I dig. I breathe as little as I can.
A uniform.
    "Sir! Request two foot advance!'
    "Foxholes every five feet! Dig in Private!"
I breathe as little as I can.
I dig. I dig in through the dead.
I'm gonna come up with earth again.
My shovel's gonna get red with earth again.
I breathe as little as I can.
I dig.
I dig in through the dead.
I'm gonna come up with earth again.
My shovel's gonna get red with earth again.
I breathe as little as I can.
I dig. I dig in through the earth.
I'm gonna come up with life again.
My shovel's gonna get red with life again.
I breathe as little as I can.
I breathe. I breathe in through the earth.
I'm gonna come up with death again.
My shovel's gonna get red with death again.

Okinawan earth. Come'on earth.
Volcanic earth. Alive earth.
In earth we hide.
In earth whatever passes as sleep.
In earth one eye open.
In earth I put my weapon down.
In earth, in earth, in earth in earth, in earth, in earth.

Come Home

Because of reasons. My son addict. This disturbs me.
Because of reasons. My son Heroin. This disturbs me.
Because of reasons. My son Crack. This disturbs me.
Because of reasons. My son stole. My son jailed.
My son questioned.
My son no answers.

I remember you, waiting for your son to come home or die.
I remember you, I remember your son, junkie,
bunkin' into brick walls,
staggerin' in the street around obstacles he saw in his way,
sweatin' on your couch, navy blue bandana around his head.

My other son. I loved him. I told him I loved him.
I made homemade ravioli. I fed his whole platoon.
He sent me pictures.
He sent me a picture of him with Vietnamese children,
He hugged them. He called them his "Rice Powered Pals."

I remember you plugging a speaker into the telephone.
When he called I remember you looking at the speaker.
I remember you, voice coming out of the still box,
voice all over the table, refrigerator, stove,
the tin ceiling you painted with Q-tips.

I remember you, metal toaster buzzing. I remember you waiting
for your sons to come home or die to come home or die
come home or die I remember you pleading to your sons to
come home.

This is the Photo of the Face of a Soldier

Before he had seen the war.
Black and white, but it has been tinted, rouged.
The suggestion on the lips and cheeks
of the color of the living.
No medals, no ribbons on the breast of the uniform, yet.
The eyes do not look at the distance, at what is not there, yet.
Boot camp, fifty-four years ago.
His head was shaved. He was put in uniform.
Pinned with a black globe with an anchor through it
like an arrow through a heart.
Took a photo of the face.
Sent the photo home.
Sent the boy to war.

This is the photo of the face of a soldier.
The greens and browns in the uniform match the hills behind him.
There is the memory of the habit of smiling at a camera.
The edges of the lips are upturned.
There is the knowledge, this may be the last photo taken.
No smile, no trace of smile at the sides of the eyes.
Along the line of the lip, only the forced edges.
The head is tilted. The eyes are squinting.
The sunlight there is too direct to be enjoyed.
The shadow has no choice but to fall in line
directly behind the soldier.
Up to his thighs that are thicker than their stomachs.
Nine Vietnamese boys stand.
It is possible there were more than nine.
The ninth boy is cut in half by the edge of the photo.

This Moon

God gave me this moon
To share with you
And be benevolent as two

God gave me this sun
So I could see you
And be benevolent as one

God gave me this earth
A place to give birth
And be benevolent as three

God gave me this sea
To teach me to roar
And be benevolent as four

God gave us these stars
To know where we are
Whether you're near or far

God gave me this street
So we could meet
And be benevolent as six

God gave me this tree
To teach me to breathe
and be benevolent as seven

God gave me this sky
To teach me to cry
and be benevolent as eight

God gave me this hour
To call all power
And be benevolent as nine

God gave me this friend
So we could mend
Our hearts and minds at
day's end

God gave me this work to do
To get me through
And be benevolent as eleven

God gave me this moon
Gave me this moon
Gave me
This Moon

Command My Soul

Command my soul to fruit to flower
Command!
Command my soul.

Command my soul 'til my last hour.
Command!
Command my soul.

Command my soul to hold heart's reign,
Rise with the winds,
Rise with the rain.
Command my soul to find love's gain.
Command!
Command my soul.

And when my breathing heart's command
Calls legs to rise and legs to stand
With call unanswered by hand or hand
Command! Command my soul!

Jumpin' With Joy

We got homegrown terrorists.
We need a revolution now raise your fists.
The companies are destroying the earth.
The companies are destroying the fish.

The butchers are jumpin' with joy
The butchers are jumpin' with joy
There's no more fish.
There's no more fish.

Capitalism Terrorism.
Poor generations of fishermen
Pelicans covered in oil.
Poor little pelicans.
Policy shenanigans.

The butchers are jumpin' with joy
The butchers are jumpin' with joy
There's no more fish.
There's no more fish.

Hu Jintao and the Caudillo open world order,
built on fossil fuels without borders
truth oil mishap murder terror
manipulations no regulations.

Waters all come around.
Wash up on every shore.
Waters all come around
Up from underground.

The butchers are jumpin' with joy
The butchers are jumpin' with joy
There's no more fish.
There's no more fish.

North Too Long

I been North too long. I been North too long.
I been North so long I forgot how to sing my song. (x2)

I forgot how to throw down,
Forgot how to do the Good Things two or three times.
I can't stay up through the night now baby,
I been North too long.
Tryin' to do things right,
Tryin' to get things done,
Tryin' to be efficient,
Expecting trains to run on time,
Takin' a number and waitin' on line,
I been North too long.
I wanna be welcomed home.

Came down South one day.
A redhead said, "You gonna stay?
I live below sea level, my swamps are estuary.
Come to the Mississippi bank with me
where ships are in the sky you'll see."
I'm talking *Sanguinaccio*. I'm talking Halellujah
Comeh chem paisana. Mangia Muffaletta Siciliana Dov'é tu soldi?
Mother Cabrini walked here.
Mother Cabrini's devotion to *Il Cuore Sacro*
Gave her *coraggio.*
"I'm talkin bout a town under water.
I'll take you on The Misery Tour.
Just show me the way to *doppia cittadinanza.*"

There's no way up but down. No way right but wrong.
Baby I been in my brain too long.
Mamma come take me home.
I gotta remember where I come from.
In the Misery Mystery and Joy.
Sorrow and Glory,
I been North too long.

Lord knows I know how to suffer.
I died Friday and twice on Saturday I was gone.
When I release my soul,
Then you'll know where I been all along.

My people came from the South in a place called *Acquaviva*.
They moved to the North to a place called Massachusetts
in the year Sacco Vanzetti.
Then they moved South to a place called the Bronx.
We behaved southern, but Lord knows, we behaved too long
Lost our Tarantism, flirted with Sufism, Santeria,
Voodoo, *Mammamia*.
I been North too long. Time to take me home.

I lit three candles on Saint Jude's altar, green, yellow, blue.
For health sanity and Lord survival. Saint Jude answered calmly,
"Annie, life is suffering, pain and misery.
And you know you got to keep on going on."
I cried, "I don't want the things of this world no longer,
I been North too long."

I been North too long. I been North too long.
I been North so long I forgot how to sing my song. (x2)

In Louisiana I know I'm a Yankee, but I been north too long.
Jambalaya. I been blamed for Columbus, blamed for Scalia,
blamed for devastation, torture, creation. White man salvation.
Lord knows I been North too long.
'Taint no plantations stainin' my bloodstream,
just *larvata schiavitú*, peons on the cotton plantation,
right next to you,
I throw a shoe at the same man as you.
I am butterfly shark and white tiger in one. *Frutta Strana*.
I'm a Yankee with a southern peasant heart and song.

I been North too long. I been North too long.
I been North so long I forgot how to sing my song. (x2)

Swampjuice

The river is high, baby, but not too high for me.
I ain't leavin town.
'Cause when I leave town baby, follow me.
It ain't no time to stick around.

New Orleans mornings are waiting for me.
Tilapia and eggs over easy is the only way to eat.
Where'yat darlin'? Our time ain't complete.
She'll build her own levees, if we let her be.

New Orleans evenings are a parade of centuries.
Spirits amble through the old streets.
Hold your best partner tightly, alligator arms close in,
Come under my *chapeau*, for swamp Cajun kissing.

The river is high. Climb the batcher with me.
I ain't leavin town.
When I leave town, follow me.
It ain't no time to stick around.

Jean Lafitte's quadroon darling's name was Madeleine.
Bayou Coquille they kept paddling,
Sending ripples to this day that ring the Superdome,
which will lift us to the sky and be our home, when
The river is neck high. Well, that's too high for me.

Step into my pirogue, we'll head to Grandpa's camp,
Where Mamma Gator pirouettes when I get too close to her nest.
She looks me in the eye, bites the beard off my chin,
Leaps over my pirogue and says, "Stay away from my youngin!"
Temperatures rising. Gotta shed your own skin.
Mamma Wata will take us all back to our kin.
Life's name was Easy.
We all lived it the same.

The Passage Of Oxygen

In every crowd I see her
I open the door
There behind the door she is standing
where for no apparent reason we meet
Face to unearned face
Face of generations
Face of farms and tender pasts
The door slams shut
Listen as she walks by

From where I stood, I could not determine my direction,
only that she was there, door opening, moving toward me,
yet it was always someone else who appeared.
Floods of breath overwhelm me. I am on the run
from my irregular heart, a strand of yellow light
like a whisper, from the first time I saw her, I knew.
She had other sounds between the pulses

Speak to me speak to me
The fear that holds the lock in place
The throat is a telephone to the heart
As if nothing had happened
as if nothing had happened
as if nothing had
The door opens, the door opens wide,
inside the door opens
The door has several hinges, a glass knob,
years of lingering on its hinge.
Listen as she walks by

This body I am shut inside
surfaces upon surfaces, without wings,
muted, closed, masked, and hiding
the passage of oxygen in brief and final tunnels.
As if skin can hold you!

That your face exists is a miracle to me
I have dreamed and dreamed the coming release of the heart.
The heart is an ocean opening
the throat is the dark way out
This is the beginning of a long story. The voice
spiraling in on itself. And still I will turn
to steel clips and bone. Just a handful
of steel clips and bone. But what of lips and eyes?
The lips and eyes that led me here,
the eyes that touch me fluid as the voice?
And other sounds between the pulses

I die to know the still loud beauty of your heart
A shell along the beach, cupping the brief wind
Worn smooth by the constant water quietly escaping
A shell along the beach, exquisitely itself,
Striated, shining, emptied
for listening.

Immediate God, adorned and ready,
I see you I rush forward.
The whole being desires to love, to stretch, to leap
toward some voluptuous brevity.
For after one ocean there is another.

With no fear I will empty the heart.
Veiled and red, the breath I've carried
Under oceans, up through openings, a pocketed desire,
The muted flames collected and hidden.
I plunge my root in through dark ground searching.

The air around you.
The air surrounds you.
Imagine being placed like a small stone or star
while eternity spins around you?
I watched her cross the room.
I smile. I smile again. I smile. I breathe.
I breathe. I breathe again. I cum. I cum again.

I cum. I sigh. I lift my lungs with rage.
I am the sun testing the levels of sea.
The flames quietly mocking the waves
the flames mocking the sea.
Her silence went on fire inside my heart.
Oxygen I was offered, an exquisite place.
Oxygen like money, and now you smiling
Who must know the contour of your own breath,
The sharp and startling angles,
Listen, as she walks by

Spirit Track

1.
Peel tar
and cement facemask off Mother Earth.
Yellow trucks revolt.
Dig up a layer of tar all over the earth.
Now only raw dirt remains, combed dirt
We need birds to come
with seeds in the winds to scatter
all over the earth

2.
Church bells six o'clock.
Ambulance lights red flickering
Traffic washes over the bell song in waves.
It sounds like *Ave Maria*
Could this miracle happen daily in my neighborhood
and I not know?
Not come to 1st and 8th every sunset
to hear these bells the traffic washes over?
Ahh the red light and with it silence.
The song plays in full and is over.
It is another moment now. Evening now.
And I must continue my way up the hill.
If I am lucky I will have tomorrow
to come listen to the bells.

3.
Come fai nel vento? How're you doing in the wind?
The wind has the rain fold in on itself
The Arctic loses an inch of ice and the sea
rises salty around young Venice
while you drive through it all.
I hope you got an early start.

4.

Grandma Rose said life is a dream
as her eyes floated into the light and time
blurred. She snapped stringabeans into a little
aluminum pot. She sewed white underwear
with white thread. She patched up my clothes when I was asleep.
Socks would be made whole and laid out in the morning
She said life is a dream.
I know how I wake up,
sometimes startled out of the images in sleep
that run like a narrative film,
other times I ease into wakefulness with growing light
or distant sounds. Sometimes I just lay there,
remembering what it was like to wake up as a child,
watching my feet grow down the bed
under the blankets as years passed.
But those memories bring me to the Bronx family
that made my lungs seize and who wants to go back there
to *cannellini* beans in cans, anchovies,
a gallon of olive oil, a desktop Saint Anthony,
a box of papers and the green hose hissing
outside *la chiesa di Monte Carmelo* every July 16th,
its neck Duct Taped up to the wall with the cardboard sign:
HOLY WATER

5.

Am I awake? Did I sleep?
One thing is certain,
you were there, in the night and morning light.
Il vento e te accanto a me.
The wind and you beside me.
A string has pulled my heart spins like a top.
The rest love is unsaid.
Your nose bone slid up my clitoris,
bone rubbed bone, hot, the ceiling blew off fast,
walls beveled in waves.
You opened gently, cried for more thrust.
Gold light bathed us

I will leave the ground soon enough.
Know I am loving you and in that love we are free,
protected, boundless,
eternal, unconditional. *Hella!* as they say, Come!
Summon my soul and she will arrive on time.
I celebrate through the lament.
Grateful for your open channel and encouragement
to get me on my spirit track.

I see you shine a billion lights
as you strut toward the car toward me.
Overcome by our connection,
I look into your eyes in all their expressiveness
plug into the electric socket of the soul
taste the soul and oceans
surrounded and filled by gold light
knowing all
will be forgotten
except this gold light we made together.

6.
There's a pulmonary nurse on the eighteenth floor
I met when I overdosed.
I wanna say, —Hey, meet me with an eighteen gauge I.V.
Start the flow of my carotid gold
remove my sutures
unclamp my belly
let my spleen grow in a trashcan on the corner
sterile caps, tegaderms,
all glorious blood transfer devices
carrying my life sustenance,
hemoglobulinic love
within cell wall integuments osmotic love
don't give a damn in bodies
and wandering souls
in racecars, airstreams,
catheterize me, tourniquet, betadine and shave
anesthetize me 'til my eyes glow with infinite mortal flame

syringe my core of marrow.
take it to your bench in the sun with pine needle hair
my marrow wants to travel into the tunnel
from my posterior ileac crest
up the spinal ladder,
out the top of my skull
the hottest skull in the universe and
machine gun stars

7.
Of my hand on the shoulder of *Nonna Rachelina*
in front of the peeling plaster wall
cracked with years when I am just starting,
Of her dress I rest my hand on
Nonnarell' La Nonn'
Rachelina Lerario,
I pull on your dress gently
Your smile wider than my hands,
I face forward to the certain future,
the curl sprung off to the side of your forehead
Of black silk that peeks out of your dress,
of your neck muscles
Of strong arms that hold me in this light even now
As I dream of your touch,
kiss the things I hear you say.
Hold me with one arm.
I am light as *il centro del pane pieno d'aria,*
the center of bread filled with air,
I know I will leave your strong shores
But you, you *Nonna*, you will, you will never leave mine.
Il tuo sorriso sara sempre sulla mia guancia, Nonna.
Your smile will always be on my cheeks, Grandma.
Ti sento. Ti vedo. Ti tocco.
I hear you. I see you. I touch you.
The cracked wall
is far behind us now.

8.
Wearing your *cappello* as the sun dips
into an orange alleyway in Hoboken,
Staten Island is a hill in the distance
coming up to Lady Liberty's knees.
Manhattan wears its sun-glistened mask on every building.
This is the pier we used to make love on, before it was a pier
when it was a slab of broken concrete dipping into the river's wave
when the edges of the city marked the start of our journeys
before the mayor made this pier fancy, paved the gay cruising spot
with fake wood for the masses to hold hands on.
A safety bar to watch the river through
And one more Nooyawkah treasured in these streets
is aborted by the landlords in this town
and knows you don't know New York 'til you live in her street
When New York is nine million
doors and you have not one key.

Notes

Triple Bypass

Written in memory of my mother's neighbors Al Paoletta and Amelia King. The phrase *"L'arancia di mattina – oro puro; nel pomeriggio – argento; di sera – piombo."* is a sfraganizze (proverb or peasant wisdom saying) my grandmother Rose told me one night when I was eating oranges. It means *"An orange in the morning is pure gold, in the afternoon is silver, at night—lead."* The phrase *"L'aglio è essenziale. L'aglio è la essenza della vita,"* was told to me by my Uncle Frank. It means, "Garlic is essential. Garlic is the essence of life."

Mom on Lorenza: Verbatim

This is a text of oral history, these words were told to me by mother Rachele Petruzzelli Lanzillotto, exactly this way.

How to Cook a Heart

This text was taken from a 1996 audio recording of a conversation between me and butcher Mario Ribaudo of Mario's Meat Specialties, Arthur Avenue Retail Market, Bronx. Journalist Lauren Thompson interviewed me and recorded my conversations as an artist-in-residence in the market. Audrey Kindred did the lay-out and we self-published these as a booklet of heart recipes and gave them out in the marketplace.

Carry My Coffee

This came out as a blues song one night when I was improvising at Sylvie's Full Moon Saloon in 92Y Tribeca, NYC. The rant is based on an oral history, words spoken to me by my aunt, and is dedicated to her.

Ballad for Joe Zito

I sing the choruses to this ballad. The song was born when I began to sing/shout "Thanks Joe" to the crowd on the site of the Triangle Fire, for the 99th memorial. The next day I received a message from Jane Fazio-Villeda, the granddaughter of Joe Zito. She told me that she was in the crowd, and that in all the years of memorials, she never heard anyone thank her grandfather. I realized he was an unsung hero, so I decided to sing him for the 100th memorial. Jane gave me a lot of the information in this ballad. Two years later I heard from Tom Mortillaro, the grandson of Gaspare Mortillaro, correcting the spelling of his grandfather's name in my ballad, and in history. I thank both Jane and Tom and hope history begins to fully honor these two brave elevator operator heroes. Joe Zito's grave is now marked with his name. I hope to learn more about Gaspare.

Girls, Girls

I wrote this song for the 99th Memorial of the Triangle Fire. Originally I sang it to the tune of Leadbelly's "Where Did You Sleep Last Night." Then as I sang it, it found its own blues rhythm.

Lunch Break
for Pamela Cotton

The Doctor's Touch
for Sanford Kempin, M.D.

Nights Like This
The song part of this came to me, as I was living it. I wrote the story immediately after.

Red Sky
I sang this poem, and it is recorded on the album *Blue Pill*, by Annie Lanzillotto Band.

E Shred
The hardest stories in life are easier to deal with when you have a rock beat behind it. This is one of those stories, that I have to sing, in full out rock.

Blue Pill
This came to me as a punk rock song, in one shot, walking at night in the quarter moon. This is the title track on the album *Blue Pill*, by Annie Lanzillotto Band.

Command My Soul
Recorded on the album *Carry My Coffee*, by Annie Lanzillotto. With cellist Lori Goldston.

This Moon
This came to me one night as a song, almost in its entirety, walking alone under the full moon, near my grandmother's peach tree. Recorded on the album *Carry My Coffee*, by Annie Lanzillotto. With cellist Lori Goldston.

Jumpin' With Joy
This is a work of oral history. My mother Rachel and I sat in the car in the rain, on the day of the BP oil leak into the Gulf of Mexico. She spoke most of these words, verbatim, to me. I took out my pencil and wrote this as a song.

North Too Long
I wrote this as a blues song, waiting in the Louis Armstrong Airport in New Orleans for writer Joanna Clapps Herman. Recorded on the album *Carry My Coffee*, by Annie Lanzillotto. With cellist Lori Goldston.

Swampjuice
This came to me in New Orleans after a hanging out with artist Nick Slie. He told me some of these things directly.

About the Author

ANNIE RACHELE LANZILLOTTO is the author of *L is for Lion: an italian bronx butch freedom memoir*, SUNY Press 2013. She is the singer/songwriter on the rock, blues, and poetry albums, *Blue Pill, Carry My Coffee*, and *Eleven Recitations*, all available on iTunes. Lanzillotto earned a BA in Medical Anthropology from Brown University, and an MFA in Writing from Sarah Lawrence College. Her writings and performances have garnered commissions, awards and grants from New York Foundation for the Arts, the Italian American Writers Association, Rockefeller Foundation, Puffin Foundation, Dancing In The Streets, Franklin Furnace Archive Inc., and Dixon Place. She has taught writing and theater as a visiting artist at Naropa University, Sarah Lawrence College and Actors Theatre of Louisville, and was a writer-in-residence at Santa Fe Arts Institute and Hedgebrook. www.annielanzillotto.com

Author photograph by Carolina Kroon © 2011.

VIA FOLIOS
A refereed book series dedicated to the culture of Italians and Italian Americans

Published by Bordighera, Inc., an independently owned not-for-profit scholarly organization, has no legal affiliation with the University of Central Florida and the John D. Calandra Italian American Institute, Queens College/CUNY.

CPSIA information can be obtained
at www.ICGtesting.com
Printed in the USA
FFOW051000140613

9 781599 540528